T0194298

simply Jesus
and You

simply Jesus

and You

Joseph M. Stowell

Multnomah Books

SIMPLY JESUS AND YOU
published by Multnomah Books
© 2006 by Dr. Joseph M. Stowell
International Standard Book Number: 978-1-60142-645-1

Cover design by Studiogearbox.com
Cover image by Jake Wyman/Getty Images
Interior design and typeset by Katherine Lloyd, The DESK

Unless otherwise indicated, Scripture quotations are from:
New American Standard Bible® © 1960, 1977, 1995
by the Lockman Foundation. Used by permission.
Other Scripture versions used:
The Holy Bible, New International Version (NIV) © 1973, 1984 by
International Bible Society, used by permission of Zondervan Publishing House
The Holy Bible, King James Version (KJV)
The Holy Bible, New Living Translation (NLT) © 1996.
Used by permission of Tyndale House Publishers, Inc. All rights reserved.
The Message © 1993 by Eugene H. Peterson
The Holy Bible, New King James Version (NKJV) © 1984 by Thomas Nelson, Inc.

Published in the United States by WaterBrook Multnomah, an imprint of the Crown
Publishing Group, a division of Random House Inc., New York.

MULTNOMAH and its mountain colophon are registered trademarks
of Random House, Inc.

For information:
MULTNOMAH BOOKS
12265 ORACLE BOULEVARD, SUITE 200. COLORADO SPRINGS, CO 80921

Library of Congress Cataloging-in-Publication Data

Stowell, Joseph M.
  Simply Jesus and you / Joseph M. Stowell.
     p. cm.
  ISBN 1-59052-579-5
  1. Christian life. 2. Jesus Christ--Person and offices. I. Title.
  BV4509.5.S852 2006
  248.4--dc22
                                                                    2005027010

147429898

Contents

— Part One —
It's All About Him

🕮 Hands down, Jesus has drawn more attention and interest than anyone who has ever breathed the air of this planet.

At this very moment, the name of Jesus is the central issue of life for millions and tens of millions in houses, apartments, markets, and high rises on every continent and in every nation.

Jesus—the *real* Jesus—appeals to the inner longings of every heart, offering both strength for today and bright hope for tomorrow. In fact, He claims to have come for that very purpose.

He not only enhances life, He replaces it, trading temporary biological life for permanent eternal life. He not only cancels hell, He guarantees heaven.

So, when we think of connecting with Him, it's no wonder that we begin to tally up in our minds all the wonderful things He will do for us. What a list! Forgiveness, peace, purpose, guidance—those are attractive offers in anyone's book! When you finally cut through the fog of pride that deceives you into thinking you can do life on your own, the first person you see in that patch of blue sky is Jesus. A compelling option? No, a clear necessity.

But what does it really mean to enter into a relationship with God's Son? What does it mean to invite Him into our lives?

Does He become one of a half dozen coping mechanisms we fall back on in times of crisis? One of many resources we plug into our lives at various times to make life all that we hope it will be?

He's more than that. So very much more.

He is God…the One we were built for in the first place. He is the emerging King of a new eternal order, and we have the unspeakable privilege of serving Him, glad subjects at the dawning of a new day. And, when we fully understand Him, we realize that He *alone* is the answer to all that we need and want.

A relationship with Jesus is not about us. It's about Him. He didn't die for us to advance His cause or hawk His wares. He died for you because He loves you, and seeks to welcome us into a growing and satisfying fellowship with Him. And it is in the confines of that fellowship that He graciously and generously bestows the blessings and benefits that only He can provide.

Maybe you already knew that.

Most likely you did.

But somehow…it all seems to get lost in the distractions and distortions of life on our own terms. We believe that we need Jesus and money. Jesus and a good job. Jesus and friends. Jesus and a marriage partner. Jesus and a good self image. Jesus and fun. And so we end up living in hot pursuit of everything but Him. Knowing that we "have Him" and that He has secured our eternity, we tip our hat to Him in a worship chorus or two and an occasional check in the offering plate and then go on to capture life as we would like it.

Let me hasten to say that Jesus has nothing against you having money, friends, marriage, and fun. *Every* good gift comes from above, James tells us. It's just that you can't have a personal experience of the kind that He offers if all of your personal agendas are competing for "first-love" territory in your heart.

Worse yet, trying to live a consistently effective life as a follower of Jesus can work against us if we're not careful. When our Christianity becomes defined by the boundaries of rules, doctrine, and church tradition, we are easily duped into believing that the essence of our relationship with Jesus is staying in the confines of what we call being "a good Christian."

And that's wrong.

In fact, it's miles from the truth.

Nothing could be further from the reality of what it means to experience Jesus in His fullness in our lives.

Paul Heibert says that for most of us, Christianity is about staying within the boundaries. Challenging that, he declares that the true essence of Christianity is Jesus at the center of it all. A true Christian (while blessing and keeping the boundaries) lives in pursuit of a deepening personal relationship with Him.

When our faith is all about the rules and regulations, then our Christianity becomes institutionalized, project and performance based, and burdensome.

It also becomes B-O-R-I-N-G.

When that happens the lure of more exciting options for life will loom large and seductive, turning our hearts away.

I've done a lot of things for Martie in our married life. I've tried to be a good husband. I've changed diapers, washed dishes, vacuumed rooms, picked up socks, and who knows how many other things. And when Martie asks me why I do all of this for her, I look as deeply into her eyes as possible and assure her that all that I do is because…I am committed to the institution of marriage.

Right? Amen?

Not really.

Important as the institution of marriage certainly is, I do all that kind of husband stuff for her…because I love her and deeply desire to satisfy her with that love.

For me, marriage is not a structure to support…it is a relationship to pursue and enjoy.

It's just like that with Jesus!

In fact that's how most of us started this adventure of faith with Him. It was Him and His love for us that won our hearts. We found Him to be wonderfully compelling and wanted more and more of Him.

And those were good days. Glorious days.

But somehow in the process of our pursuit of Him, for whatever reason, we lapsed into orbit around Him. And orbiting Jesus isn't bad. We keep Him in view and we take note that others are in orbits wider and farther out than ours. We're still in His universe, still within reach of His light and His love.

But…an orbit means you keep a certain distance. A protective distance. Because we know that if we drew to close, He might very well challenge or threaten our preferred way of life.

But Jesus doesn't look better from a distance.

And orbits through space can get lonely and empty.

…It's proximity to Jesus that satisfies.

So welcome back to the pursuit! It's an adventure that you will not regret. If your heart has told you there must be something more to following Jesus than orbiting around His brightness at a safe distance, you are right.

Take a risk…and enter into His fullness.

Chapter One

Experiencing Jesus

*Paul said that it was the throbbing ambition
of his life to experience Jesus... Is it yours?*

When my assistant told me I'd been invited to the White House, my heart picked up a little speed.

I wonder if I'll get to meet the president.

Like everyone else, I'd read a lot about him and seen him countless times in pictures and on TV. I'd followed his political career with more than a little interest. In fact, I had voted for him. If someone had asked if I knew much about him, I could have launched into a rather extensive description of his background, his political philosophy, and his policies.

But this was different.

I was on the verge of actually experiencing him. Personally.

Wearing my best navy pin-striped suit, a starched white shirt, and a "presidential" tie, I stopped long enough at the airport to get my shoes professionally shined. I could hardly keep myself from telling the man bent over my feet, *Do a good job—these shoes are headed for the White House.*

I felt sobered as I walked into the grand foyer of our president's home. *These truly are the halls of power,* I said to myself. *Behind closed doors in this very house wars have been declared—history made.*

I found myself seated on the front row in the East Room. The small gathering hushed as a commanding voice announced, "Ladies and gentlemen, the president of the United States." We stood as he walked in briskly and took his place on the low platform. I couldn't take my eyes off of him. I was in his presence and found myself intrigued by his every move. Later, in a very brief conversation, I was surprised at how engaged he seemed. If only for a moment, he looked into my eyes and gave me his attention.

Frankly, having experienced the reality of his presence, I will never view our president in the same way again. I went away wishing I could know him better.

On my way home I found myself thinking that my experience with the president is a lot like our relationship with

Jesus. We can know a lot about Him, or we can enjoy the privilege of a personal encounter. Best of all, He has already invited us to experience Him personally. The choice to respond is ours. It's a choice that determines the difference between religion as usual or the satisfaction of connecting with Jesus, the One we were created to enjoy.

🌷 We all know who Jesus is.

In the last two thousand years, no other individual has commanded such attention, honor, and respect. Our entire Western civilization—from its laws to its ethics—has been marked and molded by His teaching. For over two millennia, history's greatest works of art have centered on His life, death, and resurrection. Enduring musical masterpieces have celebrated His worth and glory. But for those who have personally embraced the liberating reality of His forgiveness of sin and hope of eternity, He is so much more.

Or…at least, He should be.

We preach and teach about His will and His ways; tell His stories by heart; celebrate Him in worship; and serve Him with enthusiasm. Yet underneath it all (if we are truly candid), there is a gnawing sense that there should be something…well, more to this relationship.

Why is it that He often feels so far away? So historical? So church related? So other? The distance between knowing about Him and experiencing Him personally is vast. And the space between these two experiences separates the spectators from intimate participants.

Think carefully. It's a pretty safe bet that if you are reading this book you know at least something about Him. You know something about Him biographically and historically.

In your more lucid moments, you might even be able to talk a little theology. But as impressive as your knowledge about Jesus may be, the unfortunate reality is that most of us stop there. Seemingly satisfied that knowing about Him is enough, we have no clue that there is more.

And there is more.

The thought of a deep richness waiting for those who get beyond knowing about Him to actually experiencing Him has either escaped us or—worse yet—has been exiled to the vague regions of religious wishful thinking.

If that's your story, get ready.

The best is yet to come.

Jesus intends for you to experience the pleasure and reassuring peace of His presence at the core of your life. He wants to be more than just another volume in your encyclopedia of biblical facts. He didn't die for you to simply strike a deal guaranteeing heaven. He died for you to make you His own and to grant you the unspeakable privilege of a growing intimacy with Him.

As Paul wrote to the early followers of Jesus…

He [God] is the one who invited you into this wonderful friendship with his Son, Jesus Christ. (1 Corinthians 1:9, NLT)

And think of this invitation that Jesus extends to all of us who will respond…

"Look! Here I stand at the door and knock. If you hear me calling and open the door, I will come in, and we will share a meal as friends." (Revelation 3:20, NLT)

This is incomparably better than an invitation to the White House. The eternal God of the universe has called us into fellowship—friendship, companionship, close contact—with His Son. Jesus never intended to connect only with your head; He lives to connect with the entire you. In fact, He sent us the Holy Spirit to make the total connection possible, and gave us His Word to show the way. And, regardless of who you are or how you have chosen to live your life, you can know the pleasure of His presence.

Up close and personal.

And just in case you think that a closer relationship with Jesus is about some kind of rigid morning routine, some tedious-but-essential religious exercise, think again. While regular Bible study and cultivating a life of prayer are indispensable, there is far more to a personal experience with Jesus.

— *It's about a deep and abiding sense of His nearness on the journey.*

— *It's about an unshakable confidence that only His abiding presence can give.*

— *It's about courage in the face of previously intimidating encounters.*

— *It's about access to wisdom and unfailing guidance.*

—*It's about a closeness that enables your spirit to commune with Him, anywhere, anytime, regardless.*

— *It's about meeting Him in places you may have never dreamed of…in the most heated of seductions, in the midst of suffering, and in acts of unflinching surrender.*

There is a marvelously mystical aspect to all this. You can't wrap words around it. You can't put it in a box and tie it up with a red ribbon. When you try to fully define it, you degrade it.

Jesus is never predictable. Just totally available. He doesn't play hide-and-seek. In fact, He consistently rewards anyone who diligently pursues Him (Hebrews 11:6). But to many of us, tasting of that reward seems so illusive. Could it be we simply don't know how to seek Him or where to find Him?

I'll never forget the frustrating experience early one Sunday morning when I was supposed to pick up an elderly relative who had come into Chicago on the train from Milwaukee. The whole purpose of the exercise was to find her and get her safely to our house. I showed up on time, but where was she? Certainly not where I thought she would be. I checked the monitor and the train was already in. With a sinking feeling in the pit of my stomach, I scoured the early morning loneliness of Union Station...to no avail.

I was about ready to leave when I happened to glance down a hallway toward the baggage area. There she was, luggage at her feet, patiently waiting for me to arrive. She'd been there all the time. And to my chagrin, she was right where she should have been! I had been looking in all the wrong places.

The great news is that Jesus is there, patiently waiting for you. In fact, He not only waits, but is also at this very moment busily pursuing you. The fact that you are reading this book is no accident, no coincidence. It's just another one of the countless ways He hopes to get your attention.

It's time to connect.

The following lines of Scripture have captured my heart in recent days. Don't skip over them. Don't let your mind wander. If you really want to experience Jesus, you must read these words slowly and thoughtfully...until they have gripped your heart.

I once thought all these things were so very important, but now I consider them worthless because of what Christ has done. Yes, everything else is worthless when compared with the priceless gain of knowing Christ Jesus my Lord. I have discarded everything else, counting it all as garbage, so that I may have Christ and become one with him. I no longer count on my own goodness or my ability to obey God's law, but I trust Christ to save me. For God's way of making us right with himself depends on faith. *As a result, I can really know Christ and experience the mighty power that raised him from the dead.* I can learn what it means to suffer with him, sharing in his death, so that, somehow, I can experience the resurrection from the dead! (Philippians 3:7–11, NLT, emphasis added)

More than any other writer, Paul spoke most passionately about experiencing Jesus. It was his singular quest in life.

Everything else became peripheral—rubbish—compared to knowing God's Son. And in this text, when he speaks of giving everything up to know Jesus, he uses the Greek word that means *to know by experience.*

But here's the thought that sets me back on my heels. Paul had already experienced Jesus in far more dramatic ways than anyone before or since. On the Damascus highway, Jesus appeared to Paul in a bolt of white fire and spoke to him in person. Sometime later, Paul found himself swept up into the "third heaven," where he had an extended season of personal experience with Jesus.

Yet what did Paul want with all his heart?

He wanted more.

He was still so taken with Jesus that the entire focus of his life was to experience more of Him. Which only proves that once you get a taste, you can never get enough of Him. Having experienced Jesus makes even the brightest treasures of life look dull by comparison.

Do you wonder if this is for you? Wonder no longer! He is at the door of your heart, wanting to come in for some serious fellowship.

Chapter Two

I'd Rather Have Jesus

*If you had to choose between Jesus
and something precious to you...some alluring
dream or tantalizing desire...I wonder,
would you choose Him?*

The meal was just about finished when I leaned over and asked
Billy Graham the question I had hoped to ask him all evening.

Martie and I had been seated next to Dr. Graham at a
dinner for the staff and board of his organization. Billy, eighty
at the time, was lucid and interesting. Wondering what he
would say about his highest joys in life, I asked, "Of all your
experiences in ministry, what have you enjoyed most?"

Then (thinking I might help him out a little), I quickly
added, "Was it your time spent with presidents and heads of
state? Or was it—"

Before I could finish my next sentence, Billy swept his hand across the tablecloth, as if to push my suggestions onto the floor.

"None of that," he said. "By far the greatest joy of my life has been my fellowship with Jesus. Hearing Him speak to me, having Him guide me, sensing His presence with me and His power through me. This has been the highest pleasure of my life!"

It was spontaneous, unscripted, and clearly unrehearsed. There wasn't even a pause.

With a life full of stellar experiences and worldwide fame behind him, it was simply Jesus who was on his mind and on his heart. His lifelong experience with Jesus had made its mark, and Billy was satisfied.

I found Billy Graham's statement that evening more than convicting. I found it motivating—right to the core of my being. With everything in me, I want what he's experienced. I find my heart saying, *If I make it to eighty, I want to say the same thing.*

Even more so when you consider the story of Chuck Templeton.

Templeton's name was practically a household word in evangelical homes in the fifties and sixties. He pastored one of Toronto's leading churches and—along with his close friend Billy Graham—helped found Youth for Christ in Canada. His extraordinary ability to communicate God's Word put him in demand on platforms all over North America.

But I don't remember him for his stellar gifts.

I remember him for his renunciation of the faith.

Evangelicals everywhere were rocked by the news that Chuck Templeton had left his church and renounced all he had previously embraced and proclaimed.

The former preacher went on to fame and fortune. He managed two of Canada's leading newspapers, worked his way into an influential position with the Canadian Broadcasting Company—and even took a run at the prime minister's office.

It had been decades since I'd thought of Chuck Templeton. So imagine my surprise when I noticed he had been interviewed by Lee Strobel in his book, *A Case for Faith.*

After reading Templeton's most recent book, *Farewell to God: My Reasons for Rejecting the Christian Faith,* Strobel caught a plane to Toronto to meet with him. Though eighty-three and in declining health, the former preacher vigorously defended his agnostic rejection of a God who claimed to be love, yet allowed suffering across the world to go unchecked.

Then, toward the end of their time together, Strobel

asked Templeton point-blank how he felt about Jesus.

Instantly, the old man softened.

He spoke in adoring terms about Jesus, concluding, "In my view, He is the most important human being who has ever existed." Then as his voice began to crack, he haltingly said, *"I…miss…Him!"* With that, Strobel writes, tears flooded Templeton's eyes, and his shoulders bobbed as he wept.

Think of it. Billy Graham and Chuck Templeton, two friends who chose radically different paths through life. And near the end of their journeys, one has found Jesus to be his most prized possession, while the other weeps for having left Him long ago.

Cynics might say that you'd expect someone like Graham to have a close walk with Jesus—and that common, ordinary folk like the rest of us can't expect to get there. But my grandmother had it as well. And she was no Billy Graham. Born of pioneer stock in Michigan, she married a frontier farmer and gave birth to her children in a drafty, second-floor corner bedroom at home. She simply kept house for her family and cooked meals for the farm hands, far away from the hustle and bustle of high society. No one but friends and family even knew her name. But I will never, never forget my grandmother's quavery voice, singing her favorite hymn as she went about her daily routines…

I come to the garden alone
While the dew is still on the roses,
And the voice I hear falling on my ear
The Son of God discloses.
And He walks with me and He talks with me
and He tells me I am His own.
And the joy we share as we tarry there,
None other has ever known.

She had tapped the secret that Billy had discovered.
And if she can, so can you.

Stepping into a deepening experience with Jesus is something more than keeping short accounts with sin in our lives. It's beyond that. It is about coming to grips with a huge barrier that stands between Jesus and you. It is the barrier of preoccupation with ourselves. In order to experience Him, we have to eliminate the competition—and the competition is us! Let me explain.

First, so there is no confusion, keeping clear ledgers in our lives is basic to experiencing Christ. As long as there is residual sin in our hearts, there will always be a distance. In His Sermon on the Mount, Jesus said, "Blessed are the pure in heart, for they shall see God" (Matthew 5:8). And the tenses in that pronouncement are not futuristic, but present.

In other words, if you are not pure in heart today, don't count on experiencing Christ in a compelling way.

It's really not complicated. If there is bitterness, unresolved anger, sensual thoughts and actions, pride, untruthfulness, or slander and gossip in your vocabulary, you're going to feel the distance. Jesus doesn't meet us on those playing fields. He'll meet us there to pull us out of the ditch of our own ways, but He won't stay there with us.

I hope you are in a quiet place where you can put this book down for a moment and think carefully about those things in your life that stand between you and Jesus. Go to your knees and open your life to His divine inspection. Pray as the psalmist prayed,

Search me, O God, and know my heart;
Try me and know my anxious thoughts;
And see if there be any hurtful way in me,
And lead me in the everlasting way.
(Psalm 139:23–24)

Don't shy away from this. He already knows about your secret thoughts and struggles. He has been grieving the distance between your heart and His. At this very instant, He is waiting for you, His cleansing mercy readily available.

Dealing with our sin is step one. But I have a hunch most of us understand that already. In fact, some of us may feel that we've been making fairly good progress in that regard.

So...why does Jesus still seem so distant?

If anyone's heart had a clean slate, we'd all probably agree that the apostle Paul qualifies for the honor. Yet Paul insists that his pursuit of a deeper experience with Jesus focuses on a distraction far more subtle than obvious sin. As he writes to the Philippians, he makes the case that we can never fully experience Jesus until we stop being absorbed with ourselves.

Chapter Three

Me or Thee?

*At some point in life, we have to
come to grips with whether "He" or "me"
is the main feature of our existence.*

At some point in life, we have to come to grips with whether "He" or "me" is the main feature of our existence.

"Daddy, are we famous?" Libby, my seven-year-old, looked up into my eyes. Famous? I was pastoring a church in a small Midwestern town at the time, and it didn't take me long to respond. "No, honey," I assured her. "We're not famous at all." She paused thoughtfully, and then with confidence and a touch of consternation, replied, "Well, we would be if more people knew about us."

Poor Libby, only seven, and already concerned with what people thought about us. With whether or not we registered on the Richter scale of public opinion.

It is something that Libby will likely wrestle with the rest of her life. She, like all of us, will spend her days struggling through the sticky web of self-absorbed perspectives. Since earliest childhood we have been very much aware of and concerned about ourselves. We mastered words like *my* and *mine* long before we knew the word for *friend* or *share*.

Now, as grown-ups, we find ourselves haunted regularly by questions like these: *Who am I? What do people think of me? Have I been sufficiently recognized for my accomplishments? How am I being treated? Does anyone care about me?*

Americans spend millions of dollars trying to get to know themselves. Books about knowing and understanding "who you really are" consistently make the bestseller lists. Obscene amounts of money go to therapists who offer to guide you on a journey through your inner self.

Frankly, can you think of a scarier thought than taking an inner journey through yourself? It's not only a scary thought, it may be an unbiblical one. If you are in the process of becoming a fully devoted follower of Christ, then life is an adventure in getting to know Jesus. And, when we live to know Him, we find that knowing Him is the key to understanding and making peace with ourselves.

Trying to discover self-worth? *You have it in Him…. He died for you!*

Plagued by failure and guilt? *He does what no one else will or can do for you.... He forgives and forgets, kills the fatted calf as heaven rejoices, and clothes you with the best robes of His righteousness.*

Searching for significance? *Search no more...you are His child. There is no greater significance than that.*

Wondering if there is any reason or purpose for you to take up space on this care-worn planet? *The mystery is unraveled in Him as He scripts your life to be lived for His glory and to reflect the radiance of His character.*

Let's face it, absorption with self is inadequate to satisfy the soul—and completely inept to solve the restless searching of our hearts. Life must be about more than getting to know ourselves. Ultimately, self-preoccupation is an empty, boring pursuit. No matter how charming, witty, or profound we may be, we were not created to enthrall ourselves with ourselves for long periods of time.

Simply put, we need Him!

I'm only in my early sixties, and I already find myself weary of the hollow memories of what few accomplishments I may have mustered in my life. My failures continue to embarrass me. The inadequacies I have carried with me since my youth still frustrate me. My insecurities still trouble my soul. And the praise of others has an increasingly hollow ring. I am tired of worrying about whether or not the sermon I preached was good enough or whether or not someone will pat me on the back for a job well done. I'm tired of worrying about what people think about me. I'm weary of the carnal feeling that sometimes haunts me when someone talks about their favorite preacher…and it's not me.

Bottom line, I just flat out get tired of me.

But I never get tired of Jesus.

After all these years, I still find Him more compelling, more engaging, more awesome, more surprising, more fulfilling, and more attractive than ever before.

I never get tired of singing His praises or of watching Him perform. I find Him to be gripping. Absorbing. Beyond comprehension. And that's why—along with Paul, my grandmother, Billy Graham, and countless others through the years—I find myself longing to know Him better.

I am becoming increasingly aware that life doesn't go on forever. When we're young, we think we're bulletproof. We live like we'll never die. But when your knees protest certain movements and your eyesight and memory begin to grow fuzzy, reality sets in. Time moves us on, and before long we all will be on the edge of life in the past tense, with most of our days in the rear view mirror.

As much as I would rather not think about it, the day is coming when I'll be sitting in the corner of some nursing home waiting for them to ring the lunch bell. And if life up to that point has been all about me, that is going to be a sad and empty day—no matter what they're serving for lunch. Why? Because all I will have will be me! Which at that point won't be much.

But…if my life has been about knowing Jesus and experiencing a deepening relationship with Him, as I sit in that corner of the nursing home waiting for the lunch bell to ring, He'll be there with me.

And He'll be more wonderful on that day than ever before. His presence will be my companion. He'll talk with me, and I won't have any trouble hearing Him when He tells me that I am His own. He'll say, "Well, Joe, you're almost home." And I'll say, "Lord, the sooner the better. I've heard Your voice through all these years, and now I can't wait to see Your face."

It's time that we all got serious about where Jesus fits in the overall picture of our lives. At some point, the sooner in life the better, we have to come to grips with whether "He" or "me" will be the main feature of our existence. Careful, it's easy to fudge—to think that you can be fully absorbed with yourself and in hot pursuit of Him at the same time. But that isn't reality. You can't have it both ways.

Paul was well aware of the radical choice he would have to make to fully experience the presence and power of Jesus in his life. For him the decision was clear. He chose Jesus.

All right, you say, but he had an edge. After all, he had literally been in the presence of Jesus Christ. Probably twice. I doubt that any of us would be interested in a self-absorbed life if we had actually met the Lord of the universe face-to-face! Fast-food hamburgers lose some of their glow after you've tied into a killer steak!

But in spite of that, he still faced the tension of getting lost in himself. Paul's résumé offered a tempting list of accomplishments that would have seduced the best of us to become fully self-absorbed. Listen to him rattle off his credentials. In the crowd he ran with, this would have been good for some multiple "wows." He writes…

> Yet I could have confidence in myself if anyone could. If others have reason for confidence in their own efforts, I have even more! For I was circumcised when I was eight days old, having been born into a pure-blooded Jewish family that is a branch of the tribe of Benjamin. So I am a real Jew if there ever was one! What's more, I was a member of the Pharisees, who demand the strictest obedience to the Jewish law. And zealous? Yes, in fact, I harshly persecuted the church. And I obeyed the Jewish law so carefully that I was never accused of any fault. (Philippians 3:4–6, NLT)

And yet…. And yet his choice is clear….

I once thought all these things were so very important, but now I consider them worthless because of
what Christ has done. Yes, everything else is worthless
when compared with the priceless gain of knowing
Christ Jesus my Lord. I have discarded everything
else, counting it all as garbage, so that I may have
Christ and become one with him. (vv. 7–9, NLT)

Hear his passion…. *You can take all the newspaper clippings, book reviews, and academic honors. Take the prized
business card, retirement watch, and bowling trophies and stuff
'em in a Dumpster. They mean less than NOTHING to me
compared to Jesus, compared to knowing Him better every day.*

Taking this step doesn't mean that we stop having what
we have, doing what we do, or being who we are. It simply
means we are no longer consumed by it all. We are consumed
instead with Jesus.

As Jesus welcomes us to lose ourselves in Him, He
reminds us, "Whoever finds his life will lose it, and whoever
loses his life for my sake will find it" (Matthew 10:39, NIV).

What an intriguing thought.

Chapter Four

Blue Ribbons

*Beware the danger of losing Jesus
in the glitter of your own goodness.*

Beware the danger of losing Jesus in the glitter of your own goodness.

What happens—what are the consequences—when followers of Christ forget that Jesus comes first, and get absorbed in themselves and their own accomplishments?

It's never a pretty picture.

My mind jumps back to an incident from junior high days. I remember standing with my buddies in the hall outside our Sunday school room. We were way too cool to get into our chairs early for class. The name of the game was hanging out in the hall to "see and be seen" as all the Sunday foot traffic went by. On this particular Sunday we spotted a visitor—a boy about our age coming down the hall toward our classroom with his mother. Since he was new, we immediately sized him up.

As he came closer, we caught a glimpse of something that clearly marked him. It was bad enough that he was coming with his mom, but what was that hanging on the lapel of his sport coat? Closer examination revealed it to be a long string of Sunday school attendance pins.

In case you didn't grow up in this kind of a church, let me bring you up to speed. If you had perfect attendance in Sunday school for one year, you received a small round metal pin that you could wear, signifying your faithfulness. If you had another perfect year, you won a wreath that went around the pin, with two small loops at the bottom. The loops were for the bars that could be attached year after year to each other if you maintained a spotless attendance record.

This boy must not have missed a Sunday since the day he was born. He looked like a little Russian general, decked out with a chestful of battle ribbons. The bars under his award pin seemed to swing as he walked. In fact, we thought that he tilted a little to the left under the weight of it all.

And what do you think? That we guys in the hallway were blown away by this kid's stellar spiritual accomplishments? That we stood in awe and stunned admiration of his impeccable Sunday school credentials?

No chance.

It was more like, *"Who does this guy think he is?"*

Obviously, it wasn't the most gracious or praiseworthy response, but it came naturally.

This was the essence of the destructive dynamic under way among first-century followers of Jesus in the city of Philippi. And if we're not careful, it easily becomes the ruling pattern in our own lives as well.

Any way you look at it, the Judaizers were trouble.

The strident teachings of this group within the early church were more than controversial. They were explosive. Simply put, the Judaizers taught that the death of Christ wasn't enough for salvation. The Lord's sacrifice on the cross did not cancel the requirements of the law and the countless demands of the Levitical system. Therefore, in their view, authentic Christians were to continue to observe sacrifices, circumcision, the Sabbath, and other aspects of the multiplicity of rules handed down by Moses. If you had the Real Deal, you would keep all the requirements of the law.

And guess who thought they were the authentic Christians?

The Judaizers.

As you might imagine, they were rather taken with themselves. They were the "true believers" with the inside scoop on what pleased God.

Never mind that their doctrine flew in the face of the apostles' teaching that Jesus fulfilled all the law and its requirements. According to countless passages in the Epistles, the new covenant in Christ made His work supreme and final—and our good works are simply a reflection of our love and allegiance to Him.

The way the Judaizers saw it, however, they were simply better than the average "loose-living" so-called Christian.

On the other side, the "faith alone" crowd looked at the Judaizers as prime examples of legalism gone amok. As the two camps began to debate, argue, and polarize, they focused on their own distinctives and rejoiced in their own doctrinal correctness.

"We've got it right, and you've got it all wrong."
"No, WE'VE got it right, and YOU'VE got it all wrong."
"No, we don't!"
"Yes, you do!"
And guess who got lost in the scuffle?

Jesus.

That suited Satan's plans perfectly. The church at Philippi was ready to self-destruct—to implode under the weight of its own intramural "Who's the Best?" tournament. The Judaizers were convinced they had won. They kept all the Law. Their work, instead of being a reflection of their love for Jesus, was a reflection of their love for themselves.

It is a strange and subtly destructive dynamic that the better we become, the more we seem to get stuck on ourselves. The demons of pride and self-adulation lurk just around the corner of every good deed. If we're not careful, the better we are, the worse we might become.

Living to flaunt your goodness or to measure yourself by everyone else may very well be the major barrier to a deepening experience of Jesus in our lives. As we have said, life cannot be about you and Him at the same time. Either you are the feature or He is. Take your pick.

In our Christian culture there are lots of fields on which to play this "look-at-me" game....

- Keeping the longest list of rules and living as though strictness is next to godliness
- Serving in high-profile positions in churches and worthy organizations
- Serving in low-profile positions in those same places
- Finding success in the marketplace
- Raising godly kids
- Home-schooling
- Not home-schooling

- Worshiping with contemporary music
- Worshiping in the traditional way
- Using newer Bible translations
- Rejecting newer Bible translations and sticking with the older ones
- Giving large amounts of money
- Getting invitations to the "right" events

The list goes on. And while we don't actually pass out blue ribbons or medals for spiritual accomplishments, we do tend to wear them in our attitudes and self-serving chatter. And when we do, we betray the secret that we've been trying to hide: that life, even when we serve Jesus, is really about "me" after all.

So what is a Jesus seeker to do? Stop being good? Stop being blessed? Stop serving? Stop obeying? Stop sacrificing and surrendering?

Obviously not. Then what are we to do?

Having learned that experiencing Jesus requires transitioning from being self-absorbed, we are now ready to begin the journey toward Him.

Read carefully.

Experiencing Jesus begins with two attitude shifts.

Chapter Five

On a Fence Post

Attitude Shift #1...REJOICE IN THE LORD.

Have you ever been around Christians who think that "rejoicing in the Lord" means wearing a twenty-four hour smile and punctuating every paragraph they utter with, "Praise the Lord"?

Do they bother you?

They bother me!

From where I sit, this sort of attitude robs our Christian life of the honest emotions of grief and appropriate anger. It robs us of the healthy emotional swings we experience day by day, hour by hour. It denies the therapy of an uncontrolled belly laugh and the cleansing of a good cry. I'm trying to figure out what these smile machines know that I don't. Maybe they've gotten their signal to be happy all the time from Paul's exhortation to "rejoice in the Lord"—which was buttressed by his follow-up statement to "rejoice in the Lord always; again I will say, rejoice!" (Philippians 3:1; 4:4).

Thankfully, when Paul opened the third chapter of Philippians with the command to "rejoice in the Lord," he wasn't asking us to go around 24/7 with a praise smile on our face. To expect anybody—much less Christians in the early church who faced excruciating persecution—to be constantly "happy" is something of a stretch.

Besides, biblical joy is never defined as an unending emotional high. Jesus wept over Lazarus, spent a season alone grieving over the brutal murder of His cousin John, and was thoroughly tested in every point even as we are.

So what did Paul mean? Given the problem of the self-inflated Judaizers and the apostle's following statements about the supremacy of knowing Christ, his conclusion is pretty clear: *It's time to stop rejoicing in ourselves and start rejoicing in Jesus.*

As we have learned, deciding not to be self-absorbed is important. But we will quickly slide back into its grip if we don't replace it with an active and aggressive pattern of rejoicing in Him.

Rejoicing in Jesus is the liberating response that frees us from the endless task of trying to satisfy and fill our souls with ourselves and our accomplishments. It frees us from the endless torment of worrying about being recognized, affirmed, and adequately appreciated. It soothes otherwise fragile egos that are quickly frustrated and irritated when others don't live up to our expectations or when we don't get what we think we "deserve."

Living to brag on Jesus instead of ourselves must have been what Jeremiah had in mind when he declared:

> This is what the LORD says: "Let not the wise man gloat in his wisdom, or the mighty man in his might, or the rich man in his riches. Let them boast in this alone: that they truly know me and understand that I am the LORD who is just and righteous, whose love is unfailing, and that I delight in these things. I, the LORD, have spoken!" (Jeremiah 9:23–24, NLT)

When you think about it, there is far more to brag about in Him than the best of what any of us could ever hope to be or accomplish. When Paul celebrated Christ's awesome list of credentials, he could hardly stop writing for the sheer joy of it all.

He was shamelessly boasting.

He went on and on.

And it felt so right!

Who is Jesus? He's the One:

…in whom we have redemption, the forgiveness of sins. And He is the image of the invisible God, the first-born of all creation. For by Him all things were created, both in the heavens and on earth, visible and invisible, whether thrones or dominions or rulers or authorities—all things have been created by Him and for Him. And He is before all things, and in Him all things hold together. He is also head of the body, the church; and He is the beginning, the first-born from the dead; so that He Himself might come to have first place in everything. (Colossians 1:14–18)

Boasting is a healthy activity when it centers on Jesus. You can introduce Him to others with as long a string of superlatives as you want. You can list His accomplishments, cite His wonderful qualities, talk constantly about His kindness and mercy and love, and sing His praises for the rest of your life.

And that would be a good thing to do, because He deserves it all.

And more.

So why do we keep drawing attention to ourselves? Why

do we want to get the credit and seek applause for our good deeds? Why do we boast in our accomplishments? Why do we keep kidding ourselves? Everything good we've ever managed to do is because of Him, accomplished in and through His grace and strength. If it weren't for Him—His grace to save me and supply my life with all I've needed to accomplish and succeed—I would be and do nothing of significance at all.

That isn't modesty or false humility. It's not "Aw, shucks." It's stark reality.

You simply cannot exaggerate when you are speaking of His worth. He belongs in the place of preeminence.

And if in your heart you have become preeminent, then He is not. It bears repeating: Either He is preeminent, or you are. To think that even the best of us can compete with Him is an embarrassing arrogance.

I'm not saying we have nothing to rejoice about in ourselves. Anyone who is anxious to please Christ and who has been gifted and blessed has a lot to feel good about. God doesn't want to deny you the sweet feel of a straight and long golf shot, a tender kiss from one you love, a contract won, an investment that succeeds, or the pleasure of a task superbly performed. Seeking Jesus by living to rejoice in Him does not require you to lapse into self-defacing, nonproductive "woe-is-me-ness."

Nevertheless, if you and I are ever going to experience Jesus in the way we long to experience Him, we need to learn how to get beyond ourselves and our achievements *to get all the way to Him*. We need to cultivate a reflex response that immediately triggers gratefulness and praise to Him for enabling us to accomplish what we do…when something good happens in life…when we've performed well and received a few strokes…when we've been acknowledged and affirmed…when our fondest dreams have come true.

When we are blessed, we need to master the response that takes that spark of joy we feel about ourselves and lets it explode into the joy of celebrating His preeminent provision and grace in our lives.

The moment you do this, you connect with Him and lose yourself in His abundant goodness.

A number of years ago, a friend of mine wrote a book he entitled, *Turtle on a Fence Post*; the story of his highly successful life. What a great title. Stop and think about it: How does a turtle ever make it to the top of a fence post?

He certainly didn't climb there.

If a turtle is on a fence post you can rest assured that someone put him there. It took a power beyond his own to place him on that lofty perch. And when you answer the question of how you got to the top of your fence post, then you'll be ready to turn from celebrating yourself and begin to celebrate Him.

Resisting the ever-present tendency to rejoice in our own preeminence demands that we learn to recognize when we are tangled in its web. Do you know what those tacky strands of webbing feel like?

- Is it your knee-jerk reaction to take credit for your accomplishments, or do you instinctively recognize and rejoice in His grace in all that you have and do?
- Are you bothered or—worse yet—bitter about the times you have been slighted, and your rights and privileges have not been respected?
- Have you ever performed for the praise of others?
- Are you prone to complain that you don't have all that you deserve, and compare yourself in self-pity to others who have more?
- Is church (really) about *you* and *your* preferences?

If this is your profile, then it should be clear why Jesus and a deepening experience with Him is at best a vague notion on your spiritual wish list. But when we live to praise Him for all that He is and master the liberating art of celebrating His

worthiness rather than our own, we have positioned ourselves
to meet Him in a way beyond what we have ever experienced
before. And it is important to note that this principle needs
to be operative in bad times as well as good.

I'm reminded of Paul's arresting comment that he had
learned how to be content in both "want" as well as "prosperity" (Philippians 4:12). In "want" we rarely think about
"rejoicing in the Lord." We usually spend great amounts of
time fretting and feeling sorry for ourselves. We torment ourselves with a sense of being cheated out of the comfort,
health, wealth, and happiness we think we deserve.

With that attitude, life is still totally about me. Big-time.
And while a little dose of that feels good for a brief moment,
we can't stay there. We've got to turn the corner. Rejoicing in
the Lord in bad times means learning to give thanks in everything (1 Thessalonians 5:18). It means that we rejoice in the
fact that a wise God gives and takes away, and we bless the
name of the Lord (Job 1:21). That we are truly rich in Him
even if we are poor in this world's goods (Revelation 2:9).
That He never leaves us or forsakes us (Hebrews 13:5–6).
That He works all things together for good (Romans 8:28).
That in our weakness He is made strong and that His grace
is abundantly sufficient (2 Corinthians 12:7–10). That it is
by His wise and overseeing permission that we have been

placed on the fence post of trouble, and that through the darkest of trials He can bring glory and good.

We have not learned how to live in pain or prosperity until we have learned how to use them as a springboard to a life of grateful praise and adoration to our Lord.

Do you really believe that whatever benefits you receive from the hand of God flow only from His grace and are completely undeserved?

Are you convinced that even in the darkest of times He is with you, that He has a purpose, and that He will not waste your sorrows?

If you answer yes to these questions, you're on your way to a closer walk with the Son of God. The psalmist tells us that He inhabits the praises of His people (Psalm 22:3, KJV). Strangely enough, it doesn't say that He inhabits our complaints or our self-serving compliments. If your heart is full of complaining or self-pity—or of self-congratulating applause—you won't experience His nearness. Positioning our lives to experience Jesus requires seeing beyond the blessings and burdens of life…to fill our hearts with Him alone. In the process, we learn the sweet skill of boasting on Him, regardless.

He inhabits the praises of His people.
Meet Him there.

Chapter Six

The Greatest Value

Attitude Shift #2...
VALUE JESUS ABOVE EVERYTHING.

Think for a minute about the things you've treasured in your life.

At age one or two, it might have been a raggy, bedraggled baby blanket that you clung to like life itself. Woe unto the person who attempted to remove it from your grasp!

At age three or four, maybe it was a stuffed animal or doll that somehow became as real and as important to you as anything else in your world.

By six or seven, it might have been that first bike. You wouldn't have traded it for anything. Maybe you had a little collection of some kind tucked away in one of your dresser drawers, or in a shoe box under your bed...pretty rocks or dolls or comic books or baseball cards or stickers or those tiny green plastic army men.

As the years rolled along, it might have been some wonderful experience you wanted to hold onto…a winning hit at a Little League game…an A on one of your papers…a lead in the school play…an invitation to join an honor society…a date with one of those cute cheerleaders or the big man on campus.

At one point in time, those things were very precious to you. You protected them and pondered them and held them tightly in your memory. They gave you delight and pleasure. They made you feel warm all over again.

But where are they now? Life goes on, doesn't it? And we move on to encounter new and more intriguing possessions and experiences. Our picture albums, basements, attics, and garages are a living testimony to the changing values in our lives.

You may have heard the story about the pranksters who broke into a hardware store. Strangely enough, they didn't steal a thing. Yet what they did created chaos of epic proportions.

They switched all the price tags.

The proprietor was unaware of anything amiss until the first customer stepped to the cash register with a claw hammer. And it rang up at $199.95. Naturally, the customer's jaw dropped. "What's that thing made out of?" he demanded. "Platinum?"

On further inspection, employees noticed that a big screen TV in the appliance section was selling for $14.95. The goods were all the same, resting on the same shelves as the night before, but the assigned values were hopelessly jumbled.

We are so prone to do that with our lives. More often than not we assign the wrong value to who we are and what we have.

The apostle Paul had the price tags right.…

The very credentials these people are waving around as something special, I'm tearing up and throwing out with the trash—along with everything else I used to take credit for. And why? Because of Christ. Yes, all the things I once thought were so important are gone from my life. Compared to the high privilege of knowing Christ Jesus as my Master, firsthand, everything I once thought I had going for me is insignificant—dog dung. I've dumped it all in the trash so that I could embrace Christ and be embraced by him.… I gave up all that inferior stuff so I could know Christ personally. (Philippians 3:7–8, 10, The Message)

There's Paul at the cash register, looking at all the price tags attached to his experiences, accomplishments, and treasures. He's got a red pen in his hand, and all those things that used to be so valuable, so precious, so terribly important to Paul, have been slashed down to zero. In fact, he's loading them up in boxes, headed for the Dumpster out back.

And what about knowing Jesus—the name Paul used to hate and assigned no value to at all? He can't even put a price on the privilege of experiencing Him. He writes Beyond Price on the tag because there's no way he can even describe how precious it is to him.

I'm reminded of a friend of ours who was an avid decorator. She had all the knack and instinct to make a room come alive. Then, in the midst of one of her decorating sprees, the doctor told her she had cancer. To that point her decorating project had her in its grip. She woke up with it every morning and fell asleep rearranging the details. Her day was consumed with fabric swatches and catalogs strewn around the house.

But on that day that she drove home from her doctor's office, the joy and fixation with that decorating project evaporated like water on a Phoenix sidewalk. Just that quickly, *life itself* had become precious. So precious that everything else that used to bring her joy was insignificant.

How often have you heard it?

— *A widower lamenting over the misplaced values that robbed him of precious time with his wife.*
— *A dad who had valued life at the office more than time at home with his young son.*
— *A working mom who treasured a promotion at work more than watching her baby girl grow up.*
— *A retiree who spent money carelessly through his working years and had nothing left for retirement.*

Getting our values straight is a critically important issue in life. And it is particularly strategic for the one seeking to experience Jesus.

In my limited experience, I've noticed two kinds of shoppers: those who check the contents listed on the side of the box for value, and those who like how the box looks. My wife, Martie, is a value shopper. She reads every label, right down to the tiny print. She compares weight to price per ounce, and when she finally throws it in the cart you can count on the fact that she has nabbed the best value.

If you value what looks good and gives you a buzz, then your heart will embrace all that is temporal and seductive.

But if you look hard and long at Jesus, if you read all that the label says about His matchless worth, then Christ will have your heart. Every time. All the time.

Perhaps you've never thought of contrasting what you value most with how you value Christ. But to experience Him in the fullness He intends, you've got to go through the exercise. And this exercise is far more than just giving mental assent to the fact that Jesus is most important. Most of us have been doing that all of our lives—and then go on to live like He was eighth or ninth on the list. *It's only when we understand why there is no one like Him and nothing else besides Him that we are able to embrace His unsurpassable value—even in the face of the fiercest of competitors.*

Our attitude change regarding what is most important to us has to be more than "church-speak." There needs to be irrefutable substance to the claim. What is the proof of His supreme value? What is it about Him that would convince our hearts that compared to Him everything else in our life is like rubbish?

There are three all-surpassing realities that Jesus brings to our life that no one else—indeed, nothing else—even hopes to offer. These qualities ascribe unprecedented value to Christ. It is these three that gripped the apostle's heart like a vise, that by comparison left the apostle counting everything else in his life as loss.

It all started at the cross.

1. IT IS AT THE CROSS THAT WE "GAIN" CHRIST (PHILIPPIANS 3:8).

If "gaining" Jesus is of substantive value, then what is it that we gain? Simply put, if you gain Him, you have all you need. Most importantly, gaining Him means gaining total and eternal forgiveness for all your sins and shortcomings—past, present, and future. There is nothing on earth that can compete with the gift of His saving grace. And the astounding reality is that *anyone* who repentantly comes to Jesus receives the irrevocable privilege of gaining Him.

One of my all-time favorite stories from the Gospels is in Luke 12. It's the account of the man who was indignant and troubled by the fact that his brother had cheated him out of his inheritance. One day, he happened to find himself in the presence of Jesus, the Nazarene. He caught the Lord's attention and complained, "Master, tell my brother to divide the inheritance with me!"

As with so many who spoke with Jesus, he got more than he bargained for in the answer. The Lord replied, "Watch out! Be on your guard against all kinds of greed; a man's life does not consist in the abundance of his possessions" (Luke 12:15, NIV). Jesus went on to tell the story of a rich and successful farmer. This man had been blessed with such a great harvest that he had to tear down all his little barns and build big ones just to store his bumper crop of grain. Inviting his friends to celebrate his good fortune, the wealthy man apparently left someone off the invitation list.

It was God.

But He showed up anyway.

On that very night, God required the wealthy farmer's soul, and all of those carefully hoarded goods went to someone else. Jesus didn't mince words about the barn-building man. He called him a fool. Not because he had been so successful, not because he had so much stuff, but because he valued it as his ultimate security and placed no value on God in his life. As Jesus said on another occasion, "What good will it be for a man if he gains the whole world, yet forfeits his soul?" (Matthew 16:26).

Bottom line? Without Jesus, all the goods and gear and gadgets this consumer culture can throw at us are just so many cheap toys; all the success in the world is of no ultimate value at all. Gaining Jesus not only settles the problem of guilt and judgment before a just and holy God, but it also showers us with an abundance of other graces with which nothing in this world can compete.

— *An incomparably rich inheritance reserved for you, which no government can tax, no thief can plunder, no terrorist can explode, and no temperamental rich uncle can revoke.*

— *Our Lord's 24/7/365 presence, so that you have nothing to fear from man, woman, angel, or demon.*

— *An Advocate in heaven who sticks up for you and pleads your case when the devil hurls accusations against you.*

— *A limitless supply of grace to help you in the time of need…and countless other unparalleled advantages.*

2. AT THE CROSS WE ARE PLACED "IN HIM" (PHILIPPIANS 3:9).

When we came to the cross we not only gained Him, we entered into the privilege of being found "in Him." This is a concept so big that it's hard to bend our minds around it. As Paul notes, being found in Him means that you and I have been wrapped in the very righteousness of Jesus Christ. Try to imagine the blinding, searing, white fire at the core of a new star blazing in the heavens. Now…what if you could take that searing radiance and just slip it over your shoulders like a robe?

That just begins to describe what it means to have the righteousness of Jesus—the perfect, sinless, spotless Lamb of God—covering all of your life.

Apart from "being found in Him," we could not approach the throne of God in prayer. We could not draw near to the majestic presence of our God without being instantly vaporized. But covered in our Lord's own righteousness, we can approach a holy God with confidence and worship Him without fear. We can share our deepest thoughts and longings, knowing that He hears and cares. And we can find grace and mercy to help us in our time of need.

In the midst of a hostile and often intimidating world, He clothes us with His own robe and guarantees our safety all the way home. To put it plainly, Jesus has you covered. As my street friends say, He's got your back! And in a relationship with a holy God, that's a very big deal!

3. HAVING JESUS AND BEING FOUND IN HIM GUARANTEES OUR RESURRECTION FROM THE DEAD (PHILIPPIANS 3:11).

By far the most popular notion today regarding life after death is reincarnation. For the life of me, I can't understand why anyone would want to come back and go through the disaster of another lifetime. But if you don't have God's Word, then all you have is the hope of some vague human recycling project.

The next stop after death is not a recycled life in a different body; it is accountability for what I have done in life, and for what I have done with Jesus and His offer of eternal life. As God's Word says, "It is appointed for men to die once and after this comes judgment" (Hebrews 9:27). But in Jesus we no longer fear that judgment day. Jesus has clearly said, "I am the resurrection and the life; he who believes in Me will live even if he dies, and everyone who lives and believes in Me will never die" (John 11:25–26).

Think of it. A free pass that shields us from judgment and opens the door to heaven, and in the darkest of days here on earth, the bright hope of endless, sorrowless joy. In Jesus we boisterously and with great confidence sing, "O DEATH, WHERE IS YOUR VICTORY? O DEATH, WHERE IS YOUR STING? Thanks be to God, who gives us the victory through our Lord Jesus Christ" (1 Corinthians 15:55, 57).

So tell me.

Is there anything you have
        anything you might hope to have
                anything you are or hope to become
                        that can compare with Jesus?

Is there anyone else to whom you are more gratefully indebted? Is there a reason—any reason at all—why He would not be more highly prized in your life than anything else or anyone else?

Think back to the day when you invited Jesus into your life as Savior and Lord. In order to receive this triple-grace-bestowed benefit we just spoke of, you had to leave all that you were and had at the foot of the cross and come with no merit of your own. Remember?

You had to tear up your list of accomplishments.

Burn your journal of good deeds.

Shred your file of newspaper clippings.

Why? Because the cross is all about Christ and Christ alone.

This is exactly the point that Paul is making. In order to gain Christ, in order to be found in Him, in order to experience resurrection from the dead, Paul had to count all things loss for the exceeding value of knowing Jesus. And so did you. It was there, at the foot of His cross, that you laid all your trophies down so that you could gain Jesus.

God has never looked at a portfolio of greatness, turned to Peter (who for some reason is always at heaven's gate), and said, "Check this out! Can you believe we get someone of this caliber as a resident in heaven? Unlock the gate! This one's a keeper!" Quite the contrary. As Scripture says, we are saved by grace through faith, and it is not of ourselves. It is a gift of God. It is not of works, because if that were so, we would spend eternity boasting about ourselves (Ephesians 2:8–9).

It is at the cross, then, that we put all our blue ribbons and trophies in a pile. We stand as it were naked before Him, pleading His mercy and grace. And instead of judging us, He touches us with His love, makes us His own, clothes us with His own perfect righteousness, and guarantees our resurrection on that final day.

Before the cross, all the value is affixed to us—all we are and have. At the cross, He alone is of supreme value.

So why, after receiving all that we have in Christ, do we dig those old trophies out of the trash heap? When did we stop clinging to the cross and start valuing our own merit again? How ludicrous, how deeply offensive it must be to Jesus when we reach back and reclaim what we gladly forfeited to gain Him—as though it were now of greater value to us again. Was He of supreme value only for the moment of salvation? Of course not. We need Him every hour of the day, with every breath we draw into our lungs.

Keep your eyes on Jesus.

Stay at the cross every day.

Remember the mercy and grace that freely flowed to cover you.

Cling to its blood-stained timbers.

Lose yourself in the glory of His amazing grace.

If you do, it won't be long until you've put "self " in its proper place—and Jesus in His.

When our attitudes have shifted to move self out of the way and to value Jesus more highly than anything we are or have, we are ready to experience Jesus in three "meeting places." He meets us in the seductions of life, in the midst of our suffering, and in the process of full surrender. These may not be places where you thought He would be.

But He is there just the same.

And He is waiting for you.

Chapter Seven

Deliver Us from Evil

Experiencing Jesus in seasons of seduction.

Temptations. All of us have them. It shouldn't be hard to think of the last time you were caught in the tension of a choice between good and evil—or even between something good and not so good.

How easy it is to utter a quick lie, just a little one, to get off the hook.

To let an offense take us all the way to a shouting match or brawl.

To let our minds become an incubator for irritations that turn into angry words and hurtful schemes of revenge. Or a playground where fantasies burrow in and begin expressing themselves in attitudes and actions.

Temptations are everywhere. They show up in moments

of victory, and they leer at us in the midst of despair. They dress like money, wear fine perfume and rich cologne, go high tech on the Internet, make anger seem sweet, and offer bitterness as a five-star luxury. Temptations lure us to give in to our doubts and to live for what seems right at the moment. They love what feels good. In short, they offer the sizzle of sin…for a season.

But for all we know about temptation, few of us have imagined that we can experience Jesus in its midst. After all, He's the sinless one. He's the one who taught us to pray, "Lead us not into temptation…." Temptation? That's Satan's territory!

Nevertheless, it's true. Temptation is one of the places where we can experience a fresh closeness with our Lord. And given the frequency of temptations in our lives, it becomes an opportunity to meet Him on a regular basis!

In a moment we will explain—or should I say, let's have Paul explain what he means when he writes, "That I may know Him and the power of His resurrection" (Philippians 3:10). But first, it's important to put meeting Jesus in times of temptation into the bigger picture of what Paul is saying.

To this point in the text, Paul has reveled in what theologians would call the *positional* blessings that we have in Jesus. If we have been to the cross, we are in the privileged *position* of having gained Christ, of being found in Him, and of being guaranteed a part in the resurrection from the dead (vv. 8–9, 11). Positional blessings are prized realities secured for us *no matter what* through the grace of His work at Calvary. Unfortunately many followers of Jesus are content to bask in what we have in Jesus without actually experiencing Jesus.

Paul, however, isn't satisfied to simply bask in these "positional" gifts. He makes it clear that gaining Jesus and being found in Him are actually intended to enable us to enjoy a real-life, day-by-day experience with Jesus.

When Paul begins verse 10 with "that I may know Him," he uses a "purpose clause." Simply put, we gain Christ and are found in Him *for the purpose* of having an experiential relationship with Him. To revel in those positional privileges without going on to experience Jesus is to abort the very purpose of the gifts!

I have a friend here in Chicago who owns a company that has skyboxes for the Cubs, the White Sox, and the Bulls. In fact, he has front-row, center-court, feet-on-the-playing-floor tickets for all of the Bulls games. In the Michael Jordan era, Bulls tickets were the most coveted commodities in town (my how the mighty have fallen!). Every year, believe it or not, I get a shot at these tickets. And what can I say? It's wonderful. Experiencing the Cubs at Wrigley

Field from the luxurious confines of a skybox or feeling the breeze generated when giant NBA players run past you at the United Center is a super-charged experience for an unrepentant sports fan.

My friend does all he can to ensure that experience for me. He checks with my schedule and sends me the tickets (sometimes with parking passes); then he'll call me and ask how I enjoyed the game. Good buddy that he is, my friend wants to know that I not only have the tickets in my hand, but that I actually show up at the game, sit in those prime seats, and revel in the experience.

How much sense would it make if I held those tickets—flashing them around and impressing everyone with my opportunity—but decided to skip the game? Not only would I be cheating myself out of a choice experience, I would be embarrassed to see my friend, lest he should ask how I liked the game. Wasting his gracious provision would be unthinkable.

It's a similar situation—only infinitely more serious—if we waste the phenomenal price that Jesus paid that we might enjoy a close and personal relationship with Him. So what's the secret? How do we activate this kind of relationship? Paul tells us we must meet Jesus in three places:

— in the power of His resurrection,

— in the fellowship of His sufferings,

— and in conformity to the image of His death.

Let's figure out how we encounter Jesus in that first meeting place—resurrection power.

THE FIRST MEETING PLACE... EXPERIENCING JESUS IN HIS RESURRECTION POWER

You might say that Paul was power hungry. But in this case it was a good thing. God wants you and me to be power hungry, too. He wants to infect us with a deep longing, insatiable hunger, and overpowering desire for power.

But not just any power. If we are hungering and thirsting for the resurrection power of Jesus Christ, we're on the road to experiencing Him in a deeper way. And believe it or not, the resurrection power of Jesus Christ is most frequently experienced in times of temptation.

It may be a little hard to get a grip on this thought because we tend to think of the Resurrection as a glorious future event. And it is certainly that. The power of the Resurrection will kick-start an eternity of unhindered joy in our fellowship with Jesus.

And that, my friend, is a power worth having.

I recall D. James Kennedy preaching about the miracle of the Resurrection. In his sermon he referenced the unfortunate turn of events for Roger Williams, the founder of Rhode Island. He was buried in a rather common setting, which led his admirers several years later to get permission to exhume his body for a burial more appropriate to their hero's image. Imagine their consternation to discover that the roots of a nearby apple tree had worked their way into the casket.

I remember Dr. Kennedy's question at that point. "What now of Roger Williams?" Or of the apples that grew. Or of the people that ate the apple pies made of apples from the tree. Or of those who had eaten the pie and were lost at sea and eaten by sharks? Just think of the miraculous power required to reassemble Roger Williams!

But the real power of the Resurrection lies in its spiritual significance—for what it accomplished in realms far more strategic than the reassembly of scattered remains.

The Resurrection is at its very essence the ultimate victory over sin, death, and hell. All the forces of evil spent their best efforts to permanently ground their Archenemy behind a massive, immovable stone—guarded by imperial guards from the most powerful empire on earth. And then, with a word from God—the merest breath—death was defeated, and sin and the forces of hell no longer held sway. Jesus lives and in Him the power of sin is rendered weak and ineffective.

This is the real power of the Resurrection. And it was hunger for this power that became a mighty longing within the heart of Paul. In it and through it, the apostle tells us, we get to experience Jesus Christ in a deeper way than we've known before.

While it is true that Jesus taught us to pray that He would not lead us into temptation, it is also true that He taught us to pray that God would deliver us from evil.

He waits in every temptation to meet you there. To take you by the hand and deliver you from the hammer blows of the hooded tormentor who lurks just behind the lure of it all.

When was the last time you looked for Jesus in the midst of a pressing temptation? Our problem is that we haven't known He is there! Most of the time we try to break the spell of sin on our own power by learning to fear the consequences, by trying to "buck up" and be good, by finding an accountability partner, or by a dozen other good but inadequate mechanisms.

But only He can deliver you.

Temptation is not foreign to Him. In the wilderness, exhausted and hungry from an extended fast, the King of creation went one-on-one with the great seducer. Jesus is no stranger to our struggles. Which is precisely why Scripture reminds us that He was tempted in every way like we are. He understands and promises to give us grace and mercy to help in our time of need (Hebrews 4:14–16).

Every temptation is a choice. A choice to satisfy our own fallen desires or to satisfy Jesus. *And He is there*—right in that crisis of choice. Learn to look for Him in the very moment that temptation moves in on your desires. And weigh the choice. He always offers something of greater value than the lure being trolled through the waters of your heart.

Need to lie to avoid a problem? Give your problem to Him. *He will help you through, and the truth you tell will reward your heart with the freedom of a clear conscience.*

Feel like cheating to get some extra cash? *He will meet all your needs—miraculously, if necessary.*

Attracted by the buzz of some sensual fulfillment? *He offers the long-term pleasure of a pure heart without damaging and polluting your soul.*

Feel the need to manipulate your way through a problem? *Simply do what is right. He will guide your footsteps and clear the way.*

With every choice you make for Him, you will have met Him there and tasted His resurrection power in your life. And as He delivers you from evil, the purity in your life will open your heart's door to increasingly sweet fellowship with Him.

A listener to our radio program, *Proclaim!*, wrote of his struggle to break the spell that Internet pornography had over his heart. He knew that with every click he was denying and distancing himself from Jesus. To remind him of the choice, he finally put a picture of Jesus in the corner of his computer screen. With that reminder of the presence of Jesus, he found it impossible to pursue those alluring sights.

In the end, most sin is about enhancing or preserving your life, reputation, pleasure, prosperity, or safety. If life is about you, sin will come easily. But if you have begun to live to rejoice in the Lord instead of in yourself, you'll be glad to meet Him in temptation and let Him take you by the hand. If you value Jesus as the preeminent value of your existence, you will never dream of trading Him for the poison porridge of hell.

As you probably know, songs have a way of starting in your head in the morning and staying with you all day. Recently I woke up singing a favorite song from years past, *"I'd rather have Jesus…than be held in sin's dread sway."* Throughout the day, as temptations ambushed my heart, the words drove me to Him.

I sing that song in my heart a lot these days! It helps me to meet Jesus in times of temptation and to keep my heart pure and open for the One who seeks to come in and dine.

Chapter Eight

The Trouble with Intimacy

Experiencing Jesus in seasons of suffering.

The transatlantic connection was filled with static, but the sound of a broken heart on the other end of the line was all too clear. It was Craig's wife, Martha. As she spoke, everything inside me felt crushed.

Craig and I grew up together. We attended the same college, played soccer together, and in fact looked so much alike that we were often mistaken for brothers. He married a pretty coed in college and after graduation enlisted in the Air Force.

I hadn't seen Craig in years. Imagine my surprise when our paths crossed in the town where I began my first pastorate. Talk had it that Craig and Martha had been far from the Lord. When Martie and I heard that they had recommitted their lives to the Lord, we were overjoyed. It wasn't long before they became active in our little church. He taught our high school boys, and Martha taught the girls. Before long, God led them to work with troubled teens on the island of Haiti.

They'd been in Haiti only a week, and now Martha was telling me that Craig had suffered a serious injury while diving into a pool. He didn't make it through the night. Martha was there alone. Less than thirty years old, and already a widow. Her dreams and hopes dashed. How could this be? Only days into a fresh commitment to serve Jesus, and nothing left to show for it but unbearable loss.

Job's comforters may not have had a lot right, but Eliphaz certainly had a point.

"Man," he said, "is born to trouble as surely as sparks fly upward" (Job 5:7, NIV).

Let's face it: Trouble happens. In fact, as a friend of mine points out, if we really understood the depth of the Fall and the grip that sin has on this world, we would be surprised that anything good happens *at all*.

The trouble with trouble is that it seems so indiscriminate.

Good people suffer. Bad people prosper. Exploiters exploit with seeming impunity. Children are victimized by crack addict parents, and elderly folks end up being neglected and marginalized.

We have a wonderful neighbor in her eighties. Charmingly crusty, with an engaging personality, she seems to enjoy being a touch out-of-sorts about some things. It's her "gig," and we love her for it. She claims that her everyday consumption of gin and cigarettes "keeps her fresh." Her sister, on the other hand, is as proper as they come. She doesn't drink or smoke. She exercises faithfully at the local pool, and she complains about nothing. Last winter, while swimming her daily routine, she was taken ill and lay in a coma in the hospital for days, until she finally died.

Our neighbor was stunned. Her sister was her only living relative. All she could say in the days following her sister's death was, "I don't understand it. *It should have been me!* My sister was such a good person."

The truth, of course, is that none of us is exempt. Jesus stated very clearly, "In this world you will have trouble" (John 16:33, NIV). And He was talking to His closest friends!

Is there anyone left on the planet who actually feels that the world is gradually getting better and better? That we are more civilized? If you harbor such thoughts, consider the horrific events surrounding September 11, 2001—or just spend a few minutes with CNN on any given night.

The good news in all this bad news is that a special experience with Jesus is there for the taking—right in the middle of that hardship.

THE SECOND MEETING PLACE...EXPERIENCING JESUS IN THE FELLOWSHIP OF HIS SUFFERINGS

Our instincts tell us to resist trouble. To fight it. To resent it as an intruder. To feel cheated. To tell ourselves, *I deserve better than this.* And as those thoughts settle in, the great scramble begins. We plot, manipulate, fret, seek revenge, doubt God and His goodness, threaten, harbor anger, flirt with bitterness, withdraw, and—if all else fails—throw a major pity party. And by the way, if you throw a pity party don't bother sending out invitations. Friends may try to cheer you up—and that would wreck everything.

Thankfully, for those of us who seek the face of God in the midst of trouble, we discover that He is not surprised by the arrival of pain—and that He wants us to experience Him there.

Paul knew that in suffering he had the opportunity to gain a deeper, more experiential knowledge of Jesus. We discover the same thing—that closer, sweeter walk—when we connect with Him in our seasons of suffering. As Paul puts it, there is a special encounter with Christ when we share in the "fellowship of His sufferings" (Philippians 3:10).

If you are thinking here of the cross, then you will struggle to meet Him in your sufferings. Most likely, none of us will be crucified—not literally. But the sufferings of Christ are far more extensive, more identifiable, than only the injustices of Golgotha.

Have you ever felt lonely, displaced, misrepresented, or misunderstood? Have you ever found yourself severely restricted? Denied of your rights and privileges? Betrayed by a close friend? Have you ever been left out of the power group and plotted against? Have you ever done right and suffered for it? Have you ever tasted the bitterness of injustice? Have you ever longed for your friends to stand with you in your moment of need, only to sense they're really too consumed with their own needs to pay much attention? Have you ever experienced unbearable pain? Have you ever felt abandoned by God?

These, and many more, are the sufferings Jesus endured on our behalf. He bore them in love, patiently and willingly for us, so that "by His wounds we are healed" (Isaiah 53:5).

If you found yourself nodding your head to any of those questions, you can identify with what He felt and suffered for you.

The question is not, Are you willing to suffer? We have

little choice about that. The real question is, Are you willing to meet Jesus there—right in the midst of your pain?

Are you willing to make that choice?

To experience Him in the midst of our pain requires that we stop whining about our trials. How often do we find our hearts complaining, *Why is He doing this to me? Does He really care? Does He truly feel the ache in my heart and the anguish in my spirit? Does He have any idea what He's putting me through?* Residual anger, revenge, bitterness, self-imposed depression, and despair are the rewards we reap from these attitudes.

Jesus has something better in mind.

If we really desire to experience Him, we need to stop blaming God, reverse our self-centered demand for release, and realize for the first time in our lives that we are getting a firsthand experience of what He felt and experienced as He suffered for us. Stop and identify the type of trouble you feel. Think through Christ's suffering and identify where His pain meets yours. Ask Him to forgive you for feeling that you should be exempt. And as you feel His pain in yours, thank Him that He loved you enough to suffer like this for you.

Stay there with Him. Refuse to let Satan draw you back into bitterness and self-pity, and you will find Jesus a meaningful companion in the midst of trouble.

We need to be deeply taken with the thought that in

suffering we understand a little of what He went through for us. And maybe, just maybe, we will begin to grasp—sand particle by sand particle—the depth of His love for us. What words cannot express in trying to explain the marvelous love of Jesus, suffering servants feel in the deepest parts of their souls.

This is the fellowship of His sufferings.

This is the intimacy of a shared experience with Jesus.

This is where He waits to meet us. It's time to stop turning our backs on Him in pain and flee to His embrace.

But we are only free to do this when we have ceased to live to rejoice in ourselves. If we are intent to celebrate "me" in life, we will resist trials and quickly become embittered when they settle in for the long haul—to say nothing of the difficulty in meeting Jesus in pain when we have valued comfort and peace more than nearness to Him. If He is the supreme value in our lives then we will be willing to meet Him in times of trouble.

When I was serving at the Moody Bible Institute, the trustees had a policy that I couldn't travel alone. When our children were at home, I often traveled with a colleague from the Institute. After I returned home, I would reenter Martie's world of runny noses, school lunches, taxi runs, and bedtime stories.

I'd try my best to brief her on the trip and tell her about all the things I had seen and the people I had met, but there really wasn't much connection. How could there be? For one thing, I'm a man. And most men like to cut to the bottom line, rather than share details. For another thing, she simply hadn't been there. After I would give my little spiel, she in turn would try to explain to me all that happened while I was gone—all the little trials and joys of caring for growing children. I did my best to enter into her experiences.

But I really couldn't. I hadn't been there.

Now, however, our children are married and have homes of their own. Happily, Martie and I often travel together. We share the experiences of new places and new faces, of sometimes stressful meetings; we watch the Lord work through the ministry of His Word and experience the joy of His work together. We experience missed connections and delightful conversation with new friends around a dinner table in some cozy restaurant.

We come home and talk about where we've been and what we've done. We relive our experiences, smile together over the funny moments, and sigh over the stories of pain and heartache we encounter along the way. It's amazing how much closer we are today in our intimacy with one another. All because of shared experiences. Our lives are no longer two worlds that periodically merge. Our worlds are the same, and we know each other better today than ever before. And we love it this way!

It's like that in our relationship with Jesus. You've got to capitalize on where your world merges with His. And suffering is one of the places where your world and His intersect. If you choose to see your season of suffering as a moment to capture a shared experience with God's Son, your intimacy with Him will become a deepening reality. It is a firsthand experience with the reality of His love for you and the heavy price He paid for your redemption.

Yes, your pain will still be pain—sometimes extremely difficult to endure. But instead of focusing on the loss, the hardship, the obstacle, you will step through the door of a fellowship beyond words to describe.

After Craig's tragic death, questions plagued us all. Why, God? Why now? Why them? But God's grace was strengthening Martha's heart. In the midst of her hurt she chose to see the suffering as a shared experience with Jesus. She wrote to me that she had decided to view her pain through His loss at the cross. She marked the loneliness and despair in her heart, recalling the loneliness and despair Jesus had experienced for her. His words, "My God, why have You forsaken me?" echoed in her soul. She found solace in Jesus' confidence that

His loss was not in vain, but that His suffering was a part of His Father's wise and bigger plan. She chose to endure the pain for the joy that was set before her, just as Jesus did (Hebrews 12).

Martha found unusual supporting grace in meeting Jesus in her loss, and it opened the door of her heart to His strong and abiding presence. Recently she wrote in reflection: "During that time of emotional recovery, God revealed Himself in ways I could not imagine. Physical, financial, emotional, and spiritual needs were met in dramatic and supernatural ways."

Today, Martha teaches a large women's Bible class, has a ministry to women in prison, and has a son who serves as a missionary. Had she not met Jesus in her sorrow, I wonder where lesser instincts might have taken her?

Chapter Nine

Sweet Surrender

Going all the way to Gethsemane.

Going all the way to Gethsemane.

Bob always said he wanted a closer walk with the Lord, but seemed continually frustrated. No matter what he did, his longing for Jesus never seemed satisfied.

His pastor had told him he couldn't really expect such a relationship this side of heaven. But Bob knew in his heart there had to be more, more than he was experiencing. What really frustrated him was that others seemed to find that closer, more intimate walk he wanted so much. So he knew it was possible. In fact, he tried so hard that at times he felt frustrated with God. He often thought that if God was truly "a rewarder of those who diligently seek Him," then He must have run out of rewards when Bob stepped up.

He tithed and then some.

He served as an elder in his church.

He regularly met with God in devotions and prayer.

He was good to his wife and spent time with his kids.

He even fasted on occasion.

What else was there to do? What, pray tell, did God expect? What did He require anyway?

Listening to Bob's complaint reminds me of the time that Israel felt the same way. In the days of the prophet Micah they filed a grievance with heaven; in fact, their whole tone seems to indicate that they were miffed about the distance God seemed to keep between Himself and them.

With what shall I come to the LORD
    And bow myself before the God on high?
Shall I come to Him with burnt offerings,
    With yearling calves?
Does the LORD take delight in thousands of rams,
    In ten thousand rivers of oil?
Shall I present my firstborn for my rebellious acts,
    The fruit of my body for the sin of my soul?
(Micah 6:6–7)

You can almost feel their frustration in the text. *What's it all about, Lord? What does it really take to sense Your nearness? Have we missed something?*

The Lord graciously responded with a reminder of what it is that He requires. He named three keys to closing the distance. (I've always been thankful that our God is a God of short lists. Imagine if He had dropped a tome of detailed requirements for us to live up to. Given His holiness, He could have done just that. But He didn't.) What is it that pleases Him? To do justice. To love mercy. To walk humbly with your God.

It was the "walk humbly with your God" that Bob had unknowingly missed. One of the basic expressions of humility is complete obedience at any cost. When I say no to God, keep an area of my life to myself, or withhold what He requires, He sees it for what it is—an act of willful pride. And as Peter reminds us, He resists the proud! (1 Peter 5:5). That sounds like a clear clue as to why some of us feel kept at arm's length from Jesus.

Letting God's people go was a tough task for Pharaoh. The Israelites comprised the heart of Egypt's labor force. They were the backbone of the economy. God had asked the Egyptian king to do something of great difficulty and phenomenal risk. When he refused, Moses said to him, "Why do you refuse to humble yourself before God?"

Jesus humbled Himself and became obedient unto death, even the death of the cross (Philippians 2:8). Which is exactly Paul's point about meeting Jesus by becoming conformed to His death (Philippians 3:10).

THE THIRD MEETING PLACE... TOTAL SURRENDER

Paul writes that the third way to experience Jesus in our lives is by a willing conformity to His death (3:10). Again, we cannot think of this in terms of the Crucifixion alone. This is not about dying so that we can get to heaven to experience Jesus there. It's about coming to grips with the dynamics of Jesus' death and conforming our lives to that pattern.

Actually, the death of Jesus began long before the cross, in eternity past when Jesus willingly surrendered to the Father's decree that He should die for the sins of the world. In our history, that surrender was reenacted in the Garden of Gethsemane. There, while His friends slept, He went through the excruciating pain of the heaviest decision of His life. His Father was asking Him to go to the cross, where the pain and torment of the sins of the world would press upon His sinless soul while soldiers mocked and curious bystanders gawked.

The Gospels record that the grief of this decision was so wrenching He literally sweated drops of blood in the process. Every sweat gland is surrounded by a whole network of tiny blood vessels; this is how our body cools itself. The moment of extreme crisis was so intense for Jesus that these vessels burst under the pressure. This decision wracked every aspect of His being. The cost was beyond measure, beyond comprehension.

It is not surprising, then, that Jesus in His humanity shrank from the horror—asking His Father if there might not be another way. But in the end, through lips parched with anxiety, in a voice heavy with the weight of the cross to come, He uttered those unforgettable words of unparalleled resolve, "Not My will, but Yours be done!" (Luke 22:42).

Being conformed to His death means *full surrender* to our Father's will—regardless. No excuses. No escape clauses. No negotiation. And not only is it surrender for the moment, it is about *persevering* in the resolve until we have fully obeyed. As an exhausted Jesus rose from His prayer, He could see the torches of the approaching lynch mob. Judas stepped forward and betrayed the Lord of life with a kiss of death. Jesus could have lashed out at Judas, blamed the whole mess on him, told the authorities that they were in league with a man whose motives were highly suspect.

But Jesus would not be deterred. When Peter unsheathed

his sword and slashed one of the servants across the face, severing the man's ear, Jesus had every right to escalate the conflict. He could have called twelve legions of angels, exercising His rights and power in the perfectly justifiable defense of innocence. Instead, He persevered in surrender. Foreshadowing what He was about to do at the cross, He loved His enemies and healed the wounded man's ear.

It's one thing to surrender. It's quite another to persevere when we're presented with opportunities to justifiably slide out of our resolve. Through all of those horrible hours to follow, when the faultlessly righteous Jesus was dragged through the halls of the kangaroo courts, He refused to return their accusations and slander.

Peter was there. He knew. Years later he would pen, "Christ also suffered for you, leaving you an example for you to follow in His steps…while being reviled, He did not revile in return; while suffering, He uttered no threats, but kept entrusting Himself to Him who judges righteously" (1 Peter 2:21, 23).

This is the pattern we are to follow in our lives if we are to know Jesus. An undaunted and nonnegotiable loyalty to Jesus—regardless of the cost—is the key to a deepening, intimate fellowship with Him. Regardless of what He requires, those who want to draw close to Him meet Him at that sweat-stained rock in the Garden and brokenly repeat His words after Him: "Not my will, but Yours be done."

It is a resolve that covers the whole waterfront of our existence. Nothing is exempt. Relationships, real estate, financial resources, spouses, children, grandchildren, desires, dreams, plans, attitudes, and actions are all included.

It calls for the bold and determined cessation of that fulfilling affair.

It demands no flirting around the edges of sensuality and the immediate resolve to eliminate opportunities for voyeuristic pleasure with pornography.

It requires the expulsion of jealousy, residual anger, and the bitterness that tears at our relationships. Gethsemane asks for it all. Stay at the rock until there is nothing held back. Then rise, take up your cross, and follow Him. Remember, no cross is heavier than His was. When we are committed to rejoicing in the Lord rather than ourselves and we value Jesus and His perfect will more than our own rights, privileges, and possessions, the cross of surrender will be an honor, not a burden.

But there is more. Think with me for a minute. We know that the theme of the cross is love. Love, in fact, for those who have deeply offended God in their sin and rebellion. And Jesus was giving His very lifeblood for these people.

He was dying for the Pharisees…who falsely accused.

He was dying for the soldiers…who were caustically cruel.

He was dying for the Sanhedrin…who broke their own laws to condemn Him.

He was dying for Pilate…who caved in to political pressure.

He was dying for Herod…who mocked and sneered.

He was dying for His executioners…who had no mercy.

He was dying for all those who throughout history past and ages to come would mock and spit in the face of His Father whom He loved.

And He was dying for me and you, while we were still in our sin and rebellion.

Simply put, the heart of the cross is about loving our enemies. It is about mercy for those who deserved nothing but retribution. It is about taking the rap for someone else, about doing justice for the unjust. Being "conformed to His death" means that I am willing to forgive those who have cruelly offended me, commit acts of love toward those who deserve my scorn, and take the rap for my enemies when necessary. I do these things understanding that God Himself will ultimately deal with my offenders in a just and righteous way. But more importantly, I conform because this is where I meet Jesus.

Why did Bob meet with such frustration and disappointment when he sought to draw near to Jesus? The answer goes way back to his boyhood days. Bob's dad had left his mother when he was young. But not so young that he didn't live with the awful memories of the cruel abuse. Bob's dad had multiple affairs with women all over town, and he finally ran off with and married his wife's best friend. He lives in a town not far from Bob, and Bob long ago vowed that he would never forgive his dad.

The risk was too great.

The fear of further rejection too strong.

The thought of dredging up old pain too daunting.

The prospect of restoring that broken relationship too great a mountain to climb.

So Bob didn't make contact. He refused to move one inch toward reconciliation. In his mind, this was the last person on earth to merit his love and forgiveness. In this area of Bob's life, so near to the center of his heart, he refused to be conformed to the image of Christ's death. He refused to kneel with Jesus in Gethsemane and face the excruciating prospect of encountering and forgiving his dad. The words *not my will but Yours be done* had not crossed Bob's lips, let alone his heart.

Jesus cannot draw near to a heart steeled against His will. Experiencing Him in the fullness of His presence requires that we go with Him to the Garden and kneel in surrender, conforming to what He did—for even the most undeserving in our lives. In that light, full surrender—*regardless of the cost*—is always sweet surrender. For it is within such surrender that we come to know and experience Jesus in deeper and fuller ways.

Actually, it all begins to make a lot of sense. If life is mostly about me, I will not always welcome His rescue in the midst of an alluring temptation. The lure of the moment will seem far too satisfying. When life is about me and the pursuit of comfort and ease, suffering will be an unwelcome intrusion to be resisted and despised. A self-absorbed life doesn't have "surrender" in its vocabulary. But when we escape the toxic fog of self-indulgence, the compelling face of Jesus comes into focus. He welcomes us to the surpassing value of intimacy with Him. When He emerges as our prized possession, no temptation will compare to the joy of unhindered fellowship with Him. No suffering will be too severe to distract us from the privilege of a shared experience with Him. And no challenge will be so demanding that we don't willingly kneel with Him in full surrender.

And so He waits for us to love and value Him more than ourselves…waits to meet us. And when we meet Him, the experience of His presence delights our soul and makes us long for more.

THE PRAYER
OF THE SEEKER

Those who experience the pleasure of His presence have made their lives *simply about Jesus.*

They live to meet Him wherever He is found: in the wilderness of Satan's attack…in the suffering that He bore because He loved us…and at that rock in Gethsemane where surrender claimed its finest hour.

Dear Lord, from the depths of my heart I ask for complete cleansing. Grant me the grace to keep self in its proper place, and to make my life simply about You. In the midst of all my routines, successes, and disappointments, help me to always rejoice in You and value You above any earthly prize. Meet me in temptation, and deliver me from evil. And if I should suffer, help me to pause to feel Your pain and love You more for the way You suffered for me. Jesus, I will live this day on bended knee by Your side in Gethsemane. What You ask I will do. Thank You for the promise that You will reward those who diligently seek You. I do seek You—with all my heart. I humbly ask that in Your good time and in Your way, You would satisfy my heart with the experience of Your presence.

In Your worthy name I pray. Amen.

Behold, I stand at the door and knock; if anyone hears My voice and opens the door, I will come in to him and will dine with him, and he with Me.

—Jesus Christ, Lord of the universe
Revelation 3:20

— PART TWO —
The Love Language of Jesus

🪷 So…life is simply about Jesus.

Is that our conclusion? Is that what this book is all about? Not quite.

A thriving relationship is never a one-way street. That's obvious from marriage—or any significant friendship. It's the same in our relationship with God's Son. The pursuit of Jesus is significantly much more than a snug, self-satisfying experience with Him. It is about your love for Him in return…a love that is expressed in ways that satisfy His soul, just as His love satisfies yours.

Did you know that the Lord Jesus has a love language? It is a scary thought that in all my activity and business and "doing" for Him, that at the end of the day He may not feel loved by me at all. All that I have done for Him, all that I have attempted in His name——keeping the rules, staying out of trouble, holding firm on doctrine—while appreciated, may not be an expression of love that actually touches His heart.

In his outstanding book, *The Five Love Languages*, author Gary Chapman advances the thought that we all grow up in homes where we learn a love language. He isolates five different ways in which we can feel loved. Many relationships struggle, he points out, because one person expresses love in terms of his particular love language, when all the while the person he seeks to love has a completely different love language—and doesn't feel loved at all.

One of the love languages, for instance, is words of affirmation. So if you grew up in a home where you were loved by your parents with affirmation, you then assume that's how everyone feels loved. But unfortunately, you married a woman who grew up in a home where the love language was gifts and acts of kindness. Finally, after months of your affirming words, your wife blurts out in frustration, "Sometimes I don't feel like you love me at all!"

You had provided words in abundance.

She was looking for thoughtful little tokens of your love.

When Martie and I were first married and economically struggling through life as seminary students, I recall stopping one evening on the way home at a florist and spending a troubling amount of money for a dozen roses. Since true love spares no expense, I swallowed hard when they told me the price and bought the roses. Upon arriving in our cramped little apartment I did the roses-behind-my-back-kiss-on-the-cheek routine and then held out the roses for her to take as an expression of love.

She smelled them, smiled, turned around and walked into the kitchen to put them in water. And I was left standing there.

Her response was polite, appreciative, but I thought that maybe she would swoon or something. You know, like they do in the movies! So I followed her into the kitchen and asked her if anything was wrong. To which she gently replied, "The roses are nice, Joe, but how much did they cost?"

I knew then that roses were not Martie's love language. As well intentioned as I had been, I'd missed the mark. And while I have more lately discovered that her love language is about things more expensive than roses, it was an important lesson for me to learn.

And, it is important for us to know what our Lord's love language really is, so that we can respond to Him in ways that touch His heart and satisfy Him as He seeks to satisfy us.

So what is His love language?

Are you ready?

It's people.

All kinds of human beings…from the least, to the loser, to the lame and the weak…to the profound needs of the rich and powerful. His heart has always been for people. And since He's not physically around to express His heart for the needs and nurture of people, He asks us to love Him by doing for them what He would do if He were here.

I know you were looking for an easier love assignment in this adventure with Him…but if you and I are indeed committed to following Him, then we need to know that His path heads straight for people.

The Story

After these things Jesus manifested Himself again to the disciples at the Sea of Tiberias, and He manifested Himself in this way. Simon Peter, and Thomas called Didymus, and Nathanael of Cana in Galilee, and the sons of Zebedee, and two others of His disciples were together. Simon Peter said to them, "I am going fishing." They said to him, "We will also come with you." They went out and got into the boat; and that night they caught nothing.

But when the day was now breaking, Jesus stood on the beach; yet the disciples did not know that it was Jesus. So Jesus said to them, "Children, you do not have any fish, do you?" They answered Him, "No." And He said to them, "Cast the net on the right-hand side of the boat and you will find a catch." So they cast, and then they were not able to haul it in because of the great number of fish. Therefore that disciple whom Jesus loved said to Peter, "It is the Lord." So when Simon Peter heard that it was the Lord, he put his outer garment on (for he was stripped for work), and threw himself into the sea. But the other disciples came in the little boat, for they were not far from the land, but about one hundred yards away, dragging the net full of fish.

So when they got out on the land, they saw a charcoal fire already laid and fish placed on it, and bread. Jesus said to them, "Bring some of the fish which you have now caught." Simon Peter went up and drew the net to land, full of large fish, a hundred and fifty-three; and although there were so many, the net was not torn. Jesus said to them, "Come and have breakfast." None of the disciples ventured to question Him, "Who are You?" knowing that it was the Lord. Jesus came and took the bread and gave it to them, and the fish likewise. This is now the third time that Jesus was manifested to the disciples, after He was raised from the dead.

So when they had finished breakfast, Jesus said to Simon Peter, "Simon, son of John, do you love Me more than these?" He said to Him, "Yes, Lord; You know that I love You." He said to him, "Tend My lambs." He said to him again a second time, "Simon, son of John, do you love Me?" He said to Him, "Yes, Lord; You know that I love You." He said to him, "Shepherd My sheep." He said to him the third time, "Simon, son of John, do you love Me?" Peter was grieved because He said to him the third time, "Do you love Me?" And he said to Him, "Lord, You know all things; You know that I love You." Jesus said to him, "Tend My sheep." (John 21:1–17)

Chapter Ten

The Ultimate Question

...And your answer is?

"I quit!"

You can say those words to your boss, your coach, or even to your personal trainer. But take my advice…don't say it to Jesus.

It's not that you won't feel like saying it. You will. Trying to make life with Jesus work in the world of people can bring anyone to the brink.

But what you must keep in mind when you're tempted to go back to life on your own terms is that Jesus will never ask you "Why?" He knows why. He spent enough time on our planet to realize how tough it gets at times. How challenging, unrewarding, and difficult people can be. How discouraging it can be to do the really hard things for God, agonizing to stay on track—while your friends sleep in the comfort of a sunset garden.

With a deep concern that carries personal implications, He will say, "I thought you loved Me!" When we are ready to bail, Jesus always takes it personally.

Following Jesus is a profound privilege—to say nothing of the confidence and security of having someone out in front of us who is wiser and stronger than we would ever hope to be. But following Him invariably means that we are headed straight for people. There is only one enterprise that Jesus cares about—just one. And that is the needs and nurture of people. That's why He has made us parents, spouses, pastors, friends, colleagues, and small group leaders. That's why we've been equipped with ears to listen, voices to encourage, exhort and reprove, arms to hug, and resources to share. That's why we've been given gifts of grace with which to serve, show mercy, teach, lead, exhort, show hospitality, give, and whatever else we can do to bless and benefit others.

People are His target!

We are the instruments that carry His love and concern to those He cares about. And that is just about everybody! So quitting means that His passion for people takes a real hit.

I know…being committed to people can be a discouraging endeavor. We get married in a glassy eyed moment of expectancy, only to realize after a while that, "this isn't working out the way I thought it would!" I don't know of a quicker way to feel like a failure than to focus on the needs and nurture of people. We go roaring into the arena of needs, only to discover that we have over-promised, under-performed, that we don't have the right answers, that we lack the energy, or find ourselves short on enthusiasm over the long haul. And then if discouragement or failure doesn't get to us, the distractions probably will. The lure of earth-side stuff and the accumulation of what we think will benefit our own needs and nurture is often a strong pull in the wrong direction. After all, it's easier to focus on our own perceived needs than the needs of others around us.

But it's just when you're feeling discouraged, just when you're feeling like a failure, or when you find yourself all but disabled by life's distractions, that Jesus shows up to ask a probing question.

"Do you love Me?"

And the question itself tips us off to the reality that reaching out to others is not really about them, or even us. It's a calling motivated and defined by our love for Jesus.

Take Peter for example. In John 21:15–17, Jesus probes Peter's heart with this question: "Simon, son of John, do you love Me?"

And Christ didn't ask just once. He asked twice. And

then yet a third time. It was like driving a nail deep into Peter's already weary soul.

If my wife, Martie, looked deeply into my eyes—with longing in her own—and said, "Do you love me?" my answer would be quick and predictable: "Of course!"

But what if she refused to be satisfied with such a reply? Suppose she asked yet again, with emotion breaking her voice, "No, I really need to know, do you *love* me?" And then, before I could get a grip on what was going on, imagine her asking me a third time, with even more urgency, "Joe…please…do you love me?"

I would know something deep was going on. It would be clear to me that under her words, something big was brewing. Something that needed my full attention.

That had to be how Peter felt as Jesus questioned him in the early morning mist on the seashore, after an exhausting—and completely fruitless—night of fishing.

You're probably aware that Jesus never asks questions because He doesn't know the answer. He asks questions to make a point—to draw out the hidden, inner issues of life, and to press us to readjust. Jesus was probing Peter's heart in the face of his recent decision to turn his back on the "people business" and return to his former career of fishing. This was the career from which Jesus had called him three short years earlier, recruiting him to a new enterprise: giving his life for people. Or, as Jesus put it, fishing for men!

Peter had bailed on Jesus, and Jesus took it personally—as He always does when we say, "I quit!" Could it be that Peter no longer loved his Lord? Or was he just totally fogged out by a dismal sense of discouragement and failure?

Christ's call to focus Peter's life on the needs and nurture of people is not an isolated moment in history. If you call yourself a follower of Jesus, it is His call in your life as well. His invitation to "follow Me" is always connected to a daily commitment to touch lives for His sake—stepping boldly and lovingly into the world of those we encounter on a daily basis. You can't have one without the other.

When Jesus came to our planet, His life was always about people. If, then, you are determined to follow Him, don't be surprised that the adventure will lead you neck-deep into the needs of people. And when you go "off calling" as Peter did, He will want to know what happened to your love for Him.

He will ask, "Do you love Me?"

If your answer is "Yes, Lord, you know that I love You"—as Peter answered—expect to hear Him say, "Then tend My lambs!"

And by the way, His concern about our love for Him and for the people He places in our lives is not an ethereal "church thought" that has a nice ring to it. His question presses us to focus our lives and resources on the passion that is closest to His heart, the most valuable commodity on this planet…*people!*

Which people? People who need the healing touch that only our acts of love can give. People who will thrive on the gift of our time and attention. People whose eternal destinies lie in the balance—this very moment. People who need to have their past mistakes canceled and their future given back to them because we have forgiven them. People who need a good word of comfort, whose lives are waiting for someone who will really care. People who need space, not suffocation; who need to be loved, not used; blessed, not manipulated; prayed for and helped, not slandered. People who need to be rescued from the snares of the evil one. People who are distressed and harassed like sheep without a shepherd.

Believe me, if you hang out with people there is no shortage of opportunities to prove to Jesus how much you love Him. People are everywhere. We are a needy bunch.

If only it were a little easier….

Jan had worked across from an empty desk for weeks. Sally, who had occupied that desk for years, had recently been promoted to the executive floor.

Quite frankly, Jan was relieved.

When she had come to the job, she was looking forward to making a few new friends. In close range at the neighboring desk, Sally was an obvious prospect. She was pretty, fun, and aggressively into office politics. It didn't take long, however, to see that this was a woman determined to move her career forward—at any cost. In short, people were only important to her if they could help her on her trajectory toward senior management.

Jan had no idea of the buzz saw she was walking into as she ventured into what she assumed was a "Christ-like relationship" with Sally.

When Sally spent too much time in the cafeteria, schmoozing with the up-and-comers, Jan willingly picked up her work. She covered for Sally when the boss called and she wasn't at her desk. Jan did whatever she could to prove to Sally that she was a trusted friend. They often went out for dinner after work. Jan listened and gave whatever input she could, as Sally would take most of the evening talking about herself and her struggles with guys.

Jan was a new follower of Jesus. Soon after becoming a Christian, she had learned that to authenticate her love and relationship with her Lord, she needed to intentionally climb out of her own world and become involved in the lives of others. Sally, in her mind, was a prime opportunity to do just that. In fact, Jan often prayed that her interest in and support for Sally might lead Sally to become interested in a relationship with Jesus.

Jan was good at what she did in the office. In fact it wasn't long before the "powers that be" began to target her for corporate advancement. The thought of this was too much for Sally, and she began to look at Jan differently—as a threat to her career dreams. After two years of building their friendship, Jan overheard a conversation between Sally and the boss that shocked her to the core. In a sad, reluctant voice, Sally explained how much of Jan's work she'd had to pick up and correct before it could be submitted. Jan, Sally said, spent too much time with friends on the phone, and when corrected for it would always have a few choice comments about the weird way that upper management ran the business.

None of it was true.

But Sally had been clever enough to work the system, and it was Sally who got the promotion. Jan was stuck at the same desk with a tarnished reputation.

In Jan's mind, this thing about loving Jesus by reaching out to people hadn't worked out the way she thought it would. As it turned out, people weren't simply needy, they were dangerous. She had been used, hurt, and discarded. Deeply discouraged—not only with people, but with Jesus who had asked her to get sacrificially involved with others—Jan was now determined to take life into her own hands. She would manage whomever landed at Sally's desk in a way that would guarantee her own safety and personal advance in the corporation.

Jan's heart was no longer ready to reach out for Jesus' sake. She had learned her lesson the hard way. It was now time for her to get on the corporate train and make something of her life. She would play everything close to her vest, and keep everything on a professional level aimed at her own best interest. Life was too short, she told herself, and she didn't need the grief of another people disaster in her life.

It wasn't that she was ready to totally deny Jesus. She still gladly attended her weekly small group meetings, worshiped with enthusiasm on Sunday, and took copious notes as the pastor shared his heart. It's just that Jan had become a little more savvy in the marketplace. Jesus would just have to understand that. His way didn't really work at the office. She even wondered if perhaps the world of two thousand years ago was nicer than "office world," and that if Jesus were here today He too might revise some of His thoughts about the place and importance of people.

So, when Heather replaced Sally at the nearby desk, Jan was ready.

Heather was pleasant, easy to be around, and openly friendly to Jan. It crossed Jan's mind that Sally was like that in the beginning as well. What Jan *didn't* know was that Heather was close to a transition point in life. She had recently been deeply impressed by the unconditional love and concern of a couple of Christian friends. When Heather heard through the office grapevine that Jan was a Christian, she was secretly pleased. She was anxious to experience another relationship that would bless her with the selfless love she had experienced from her other friends. In fact, Heather had often thought (though she didn't let on to her friends) that Jesus was becoming increasingly attractive to her. She was drawn by their talk of His sacrificial and forgiving love. She had experienced it from them, and knew deep down how much she needed to be forgiven.

Warmly and expectantly, Heather made attempts to get to know Jan. She would ask, "Could we go on break together? Or how about lunch?" But Jan made sure that she was always busy. Conversations were polite, but Jan's brief answers guaranteed that they didn't get much traction.

Jan felt good about the distance.

Jan had no clue.

Countless followers of Jesus, like Jan, have "had it" with people.

— *Wives jilted by faithless husbands.*
— *Men embittered by game-playing women.*
— *Children deeply disappointed by parents.*
— *Parents stinging from rejection by their own children.*
— *Customers cheated by fellow Christians in the business world.*
— *Teenage girls sexually molested by an abusive dad—who also happened to be an elder in the church.*
— *People tired of dead-end, nonreciprocal, one-way relationships.*
— *Wounded people who have been betrayed by a friend.*
— *People who find life easier to manage when lived on their own terms.*
— *People who have found that most people are nice, but not necessary.*

The list goes on. At one time or another, all of us have found our fellow human beings to be disappointing and discouraging. Most of us feel like "amening" the philosopher who wrote, "The more I get to know people, the more I like my dog!"

So…forgetting that our purpose in life is to prove our love to Jesus by staying involved in the lives of others for their good (even if it costs us something), we tend to do what Peter did…bail on Jesus and recoil into the tidy comfort of life on our own terms.

Chapter Eleven

Ready to Quit

Living with the urge to give up on people.

I have a confession to make. I am not the kind of person who tends to find people to be a problem. I am an unrepentant, hopelessly addicted people-person!

I know. That confession is a turnoff to those of you who view my personality type with a measure of disdain. I understand. But for reasons best known to Himself, God has sprinkled folks like me throughout the world—people who feed on interaction with other humans.

If the truth were known, however, we people-persons find others satisfying to us as long as those "others" feed our appetites for attention and affirmation. We tend not to listen well, unless the conversation is about us. We overpromise and underperform. Any sacrificial extensions of our time and resources that don't reward us will rarely be attempted again. In fact (though we would be the last to admit it), we can actually neglect the legitimate needs of others—including our own family—when our people need is being satisfied with someone else. And when the current company we're in causes us more hassle than they're worth, we have been known to move on to more interesting people.

What really lies under the outer layers of a people-person (if we aren't careful), is the full-blown capacity to use others for our own emotional satisfaction, instead of truly loving others to prove our love for Christ.

In the end, people-persons are just as liable to avoid significant and sacrificial interaction with members of the human family as your favorite recluse.

None of us are exempt. We are costrugglers in a battle to stay "on calling" as followers of Jesus.

I've always been fascinated by the triple interrogation that Jesus put Peter through in John 21. Actually, convicted might be a more accurate description of how I feel.

Imagine a face-to-face encounter with Jesus, the almighty Creator, who keeps asking you a single question with that penetrating gaze that cuts to the very depths of your soul.

The question?

"Do you love Me?"

What was Jesus after?

Jesus was after Peter's love.

What was Peter's problem?

Peter had had it with life on Jesus' terms!

And isn't that exactly our dilemma when people prove to be less rewarding than we thought they would be? Peter had just flat-out become *discouraged* as a follower of Jesus.

Actually, Peter had had it with just about everyone. Including the Lord! Before His death and resurrection, Jesus had been with Peter and the disciples 24/7/365. All of Peter's hopes had been pegged on the Teacher from Galilee. He had given up a prosperous career in fishing to follow Jesus into the world of people. He could remember with such clarity the day when Jesus called to him: "Follow Me, and I will make you a fisher of men!"

For three years, Peter basked in the passionate love that Jesus poured out to people of all kinds. From prostitutes to princes, outcasts to the highly connected, lepers to doctors, children and women. His whole world was about people, their needs, and their transition into His kingdom.

Then the dream exploded.

Jesus had gotten them all in trouble by agitating the authorities to the point of a mob action against Him.

After the resurrection, Peter thought that it would be back to the way it used to be. But that never materialized. Before Jesus questioned Peter on that morning by the sea, He had only shown up twice. Things just weren't turning out like Peter thought they should. (Ever feel that way in your walk with Jesus?)

And this thing about being in the enterprise of people…that seemed to be in the tank as well. Who would want anything to do with followers of Jesus now that He had died as a disgraced criminal rather than conquering as a victorious King?

For most people, the resurrection was no more than a rumor. The "headliner" was out of public circulation, and the crowds had long ago dispersed. To make matters worse, the authorities were still "ticked" about the near insurrection Jesus had caused. And the disciples were being accused of stealing His body.

The risks of being in the people business were just too high, and the list of reasons to bail was long.

On top of all that, Peter wasn't feeling too good about himself the morning that Jesus showed up on the beach. How could he forget his total collapse in Caiaphas's courtyard when pressed about his association with Jesus?

The more he thought about it, the more he realized he just wasn't cut out for the calling of Christ in his life. People and their needs would just have to take second place! Peter was going fishing—and taking Thomas, James, John,

Nathaniel, and two other disciples with him as partners in his fledgling business. It was back to life as usual. Back to something he could control. Back to the well-practiced tasks of catching, counting, and selling fish. Back to the comfortable routine of repairing boats and mending nets.

In simple terms, Peter said, "I quit!"

You know the feeling. How often have you just wanted to quit? Quit parenting. Quit the hassle of a difficult marriage. Quit trying to communicate with that cantankerous coworker. Quit being so nice to people who aren't all that nice to you. Quit leading your small group. Quit the challenges of following Jesus into the lives of needy, fickle, ungrateful, demanding, critical, consuming people. Quit forgiving. Quit giving people "the benefit of the doubt."

More subtly, as we continue to go though the motions, a lot of us have already quit inside. We dutifully live out our marriage obligations, parent, help others, and perform our routines with a sense of grumpy obligation. We spend our mental energy dreaming of a better life. We are tempted to flirt around the edges of an affair, lose ourselves in a novel, or escape into the fantasy universe of the Web. What we really want is life on our own terms. A life where we can be in control, and manage the outcomes to our own satisfaction. A life where others care about us instead of our having to care about them.

If you are now or have ever been gripped by thoughts like these, take heart! You are not alone.

It's exactly where Peter was on the night when he and his buddies climbed back into the old fishing boat. Compared to the recent disappointments of following Christ, the thought of fishing had a compelling draw. You can almost hear Peter thinking, *At least this is something I can succeed at.*

Think again. Peter was soon to find out that life on our own terms is ultimately a hollow and futile endeavor.

That very first night of fishing they caught nothing. It's no big deal if you get "skunked" on vacation, but if it's the first day of your new business, it's a major blow. If Peter had been discouraged before, he must have been devastated by the time the morning sun sent its first tentative rays across the sea.

Mark it down. It is no coincidence that in the midst of Peter's discouragement and emptiness of life, Jesus showed up on the beach. The Lord who had called him, called him once again, urging him back to the mission that he had given up on. Back to the sometimes messy and always challenging business of shepherding people. But more importantly, back into a love relationship with Him.

As I type these words into my laptop, buckled into my seat thirty-five thousand feet over the Atlantic, I find my heart praying for you. Praying that as you read these words you will slow down and sense that Jesus is right now showing up on the beach of your heart. Calling you to follow Him once again. Calling to you in the midst of your reasons to quit, discouragements, and failures. Calling you back to Himself. Back to the passion that drives His heart to this day…the needs and nurture of people.

You've got to be struck by the fact that Jesus didn't show up that morning as the divine taskmaster, sternly informing Peter that he was AWOL, and that he needed to get back to kingdom work. In Jesus' mind, the central issue was not about the task. It was about Peter's love for Him.

Every time we find ourselves ready to bail, we must remind ourselves that the people business is not about the duty of it all, but about our love for Him. This is why Jesus takes it personally when we climb back into our own self-centered world.

By the way, if you think this story is just about an important guy in the history of the church and his struggle two thousand years ago, think again! His significance is as strategic as your own eternal destiny. If Peter hadn't been able to get this issue straightened out, it is possible that you and I would not be holding this book in our hands…with hell canceled and heaven guaranteed. Peter's diversion off mission and back to his previous occupation threatened the intended spread of the gospel to all the known world.

It is safe to say that someone else's well-being—and per-haps their eternal destiny—lies in the balances of your response to Christ's final question to Peter.

Chapter Twelve

Moment of Decision

...Rescue the perishing.

Gary sprawled facedown on the ground, pleading with the armed guard to let him into the room. All he could see beyond the doorway, beyond the firmly planted boots of the guard, were his wife's motionless feet. And the blood.

In that moment, with his face in the dirt, shaking under the crushing blow of this horror, he knew that he must decide. Would he, could he, forgive the terrorist who had shot Bonnie three times in the face? Or would he vow revenge for her blood—even if it took him the rest of his life?

Gary and Bonnie met as college students at Moody Bible Institute. Following graduation and marriage, they committed their lives to take the good news of Jesus to people in one of the more dangerous spots in the world, Sidon, Lebanon.

Although they knew it was not a safe place, Gary had never expected—could never have anticipated—*this*.

Bonnie had left early in the morning of November 21, 2002, to open the clinic where she cared for and ministered to the children of refugees. Hearing a knock at the door, she opened it to the flashing image of a pistol that fired its lethal shots at point-blank range into her face, immediately extinguishing her life. She dropped to the floor, a young, modern-day martyr.

Moments later the phone rang in Gary's bedroom, waking him after a late night of ministry. The panicked voice on the other end of the line was almost unintelligible. The only thing he could understand was that something terrible had happened, and that he needed to get to the clinic as quickly as possible. Searching frantically for enough change to pay for a cab, he left their apartment and arrived at the clinic where his worst fears were confirmed. He raced to the front door only to be restrained from entry by the police—and fell to the ground sobbing and begging to see her.

It was then that something extraordinary happened. Even while the confusion of a thousand thoughts swirled in his head, Gary experienced a moment of spiritual clarity. It was as though the black, churning clouds suddenly parted—just for the briefest moment—allowing a shaft of sunlight to pierce the distress and numbing sorrow. Facedown in the dirt, he told the Lord that he would not abandon the call to which he and Bonnie had committed themselves. He would stay the course, and he would forgive the people who had planned and perpetrated this unspeakable act.

It was a high-stakes moment. On earth and in heaven. Would Gary stay on mission? God had clearly called him to the needs of the Lebanese people, and he had answered that call…now at great expense.

The feelings that shot through Gary's mind that terrible morning—the compelling seduction of revenge, hate, and despair—threatened the very calling of God on this young man's life. It threatened the ongoing viability of the power of the gospel through him. And that is no small matter.

Whether or not Gary was aware of it, his wife was a casualty of the incessant, unseen struggles between the forces of hell and the kingdom of light. The monstrous murder of his precious wife at the hands of terrorists was simply one of hell's strategies to frustrate and derail the work of God in that troubled corner of the world.

But it wasn't the only strategy.

In fact, the warfare would not end with Bonnie's demise. Phase two in the battle would be to discourage and distract Gary with self-defeating attitudes of self-pity, revenge, and hate. What a great opportunity to get Gary tangled up in the web of the "blame God" game. Gary's failure at this moment...though understandable...would complete the victory for Satan and his legions. The underworld, well aware that their best moments are turned against them by undaunted followers of Jesus, wanted Gary's heart as well as Bonnie's life.

But they lost.

Gary stood his ground.

They couldn't have his heart. He would not let that happen. So he did for the murderers what Jesus had done for him. He forgave them. What they needed most was not Gary's wrath, but his forgiveness—and even more important, the eternal cleansing of the Great Forgiving One. Gary vowed to offer himself afresh to God—with whatever strength he had left in his life. He committed himself to bringing the healing and redemption of Christ to people in need. Regardless. Wherever.

To this day, Gary's resolve remains as fresh as it was in that excruciating moment when his world caved in. As a result, Bonnie's death has been used to motivate thousands of young college students to understand the gravity of their calling as they move into their worlds as redemptive healers. These students are learning, as Bonnie knew so well, that above everything else, no matter where they find themselves, it is people who matter.

What kind of people? People who need to be shepherded toward Jesus. People who need rescue, direction, and hope in the crossfire of a raging battle between heaven and hell. People whom Satan would gladly destroy in his frantic efforts to defame God, and hijack His eternal purpose.

There is one pivotal reality generally lost on most of us who live relatively comfortable and affluent lives. It is this…*we are at war!* Not in Iraq or some far-flung terrorist camp. But a right-here-in-our-own-heart war. A war fought against unseen forces literally hell-bent against us—and everyone around us, for that matter. None of us is exempt. The battle rages!

In his book, *Waking the Dead*, John Eldredge writes:

Here is something set against us…. How I've missed this for so long is a mystery to me. Maybe I've overlooked it; maybe I've chosen not to see. We are at war…. This is not Eden…. The world in which we live is a combat zone, a violent clash of kingdoms, a bitter struggle unto the death…. You were born into a world at war and you will live all your days in the midst of a great battle, involving all the forces of heaven and hell and played out here on earth.

Of course, that's what the apostle Paul wanted us to know when he called us to…

Be strong in the Lord and in the strength of His might. Put on the full armor of God, so that you will be able to stand firm against the schemes of the devil. For our struggle is not against flesh and blood, but against the rulers, against the powers, against the world forces of this darkness, against the spiritual forces of wickedness in the heavenly places. Therefore, take up the full armor of God, so that you will be able to resist in the evil day, and having done everything, to stand firm. (Ephesians 6:10–13)

When we wake up to the reality of this war—like frightened people who have just heard an air-raid siren—we are most prone to dive into our spiritual bomb shelters. Scrambling to find a book, a scheme, or a strategy to help us survive personally, we focus all of our efforts toward making it to the Promised Land unscathed. As important as that may be, it lacks an understanding of the extent of our calling in the midst of this cosmic struggle.

What about the others around us?

Is this really an every-man-for-himself affair?

Casualties are in the making all around us. From our spouses to our friends, our children, our spiritual leaders, those we work with and come into casual relationships with.

The issue is…do we care? Will any of us make an effort to lend a helping hand; to support, shield, or rescue?

In fact, Paul ended his treatise on the war and its armor by asking the Ephesians to, "be on the alert with all perseverance and petition for all the saints, and pray on my behalf" (6:18–19). In Galatians he writes, "If a man is overtaken in any trespass, you who are spiritual restore such a one in a spirit of gentleness…. Bear one another's burdens" (Galatians 6:1–2, NKJV).

This battle is not just about me. It is not about you. It's about us!

Throughout the history of warfare, medals of honor have been awarded to those who have distinguished themselves by risking their own lives to rescue a wounded comrade through heavy fire. These medals come in many shapes and sizes, but ours is in the shape of a bloodstained cross. For it was our leader Jesus who made a way for us to escape to safety as He threw Himself into harm's way to rescue unworthy sinners like you and me from the death grip of Beelzebub, prince of darkness.

And it's not always risking something big in a high-stakes people crisis. Sometimes—in fact, more often—it's about passing a piece of bread to a fellow soldier in need as you sit in the trenches of everyday life. An encouraging word. A note in the mail. Holding friends accountable. Giving the gift of forgiveness. Patience and long-suffering with their faults and struggles.

An assurance of regular prayer on their behalf. Babysitting.

Throughout my ministry life many have said to me, "I pray for you regularly." Some, recognizing that spiritual leaders are often special targets in the warfare, tell me they hold me up in prayer every single day. Sometimes as I fall into bed at night, I wonder how I got through the day with all of its challenges unscathed. Sometimes I reflect on a temptation of word, thought, or deed that I refused to give in to. When I wonder how I made it through, I remember my fellow soldiers who stayed on calling, and at some time that day pled for my safety and survival.

Ministry is a fast-paced, busy, multitasked affair. So is your life, I am sure. But the demands of serving God and His people can distract us from our priorities, and threaten some of our most valued and important relationships in our lives. Back in the busiest days of our pastoring, I remember people in our church who would babysit our children—so that Martie and I could get away for a couple of days to regroup and deepen our love for each other. These willing child care experts invested in guarding our hearts against the possibility of a faltering marriage.

In those early days when all our money was obligated before we got it, dinner out meant some generic fast-food experience. Except when Bill and Dorothy Eidson would call us and take us out for a posh steak dinner! The encouragement helped to prepare us to serve another day.

Let's face it, when life is about over, it won't be how successful or satisfied you have been with yourself that will provide the most rewarding memories and experiences. It will be what you have done for others that will fill your heart with a sense of worth and value.

At the end of the day (or the end of life), it is people who will be the source of your greatest reward…or your deepest regret. And what you do with this book—more important, what you do with the call of Jesus on your life—will determine how great that reward…or how profound that regret.

This book is about being in the business of people and staying with it.

For Jesus' sake.

Few of us will ever come close to facing the deep issues that Gary faced in that terrible moment of decisive victory. But if you are reading this book as a follower of Jesus, the dynamics of that moment flash across the screen of your life on a daily basis. The call of Christ on all of our lives is to intervene for His sake in the lives of people. People who are vulnerable in the conflict or being taken down in the warfare. Each day we live we are offered an opportunity to play a part in that struggle.

The choice to make a difference is always there, waiting to

be seized. The choice to respond with grace and patience to grumpy, critical, offensive, or threatening people in our lives. The choice to refuse viewing others as pawns in the pursuit of our dreams and desires, or as objects of our own pleasure. The choice to forgive cruel or even unintended offenses. The choice to master the art of loving our enemies and extending grace to the undeserving. The choice to be high on compassion and low on consternation. High on mercy and low on mad. High on generosity and low on greed.

We cannot miss the fact that when Jesus called Peter, Andrew, and the other fishermen, James and John, He made it clear that He intended to reengineer their calling in life. From that day forward, their priority would transfer from the enterprise of catching fish to serving people—their needs and their eternal destinies.

Jesus understood the awesome dimensions and implications of that shift in focus. He knew how desperately people needed what He had to offer: rescue, healing, redemption, reconciliation, peace, and life. He also knew—in a way that His disciples could never know—that without intervention these same people would live out their lives as helpless pawns of the destroyer.

Chapter Thirteen

Embracing the Call (Again)

...Three steps from fish to Jesus.

Let's be fair with Peter.

This drift off calling was clearly about more than his crushing discouragement with people and his feelings of failure. His "back to fishing" choice was also about some very pressing needs in his life.

Inevitably, in the people business, you will hear your heart cry, "Hey, what about me?" At that point, if you're not careful, you may find yourself scrambling to meet your own needs at the expense of others. You will forget that Jesus has promised to care for your needs as you serve Him.

Peter went back to his career of fishing for all the reasons we have been learning…but among them was the reality that he and the disciples were broke!

Judas had absconded with the treasury. What were the disciples supposed to do? Where would they get money to carry on the ministry? And Jesus? Well, no one had seen much of Him lately. It was becoming increasingly clear that there wasn't going to be any more feeding of the five thousand—let alone the leftover eleven.

Nothing seemed very certain or very clear in those strange, strained days. Ah, but fish…the fish were still there in the sea, waiting to be caught and cashed out. Like always.

For Peter, fish were now the necessity. Providing for the next meal and having enough money to buy what they needed for life now became paramount to the disciples.

Watch out for the "necessities" of life. In our pursuit of the good life, the list of necessities can become distorted real fast. What we think is necessary may be far less important than the needs of those around us. In fact, what seems necessary to us may actually be a luxury compared to strategic opportunities to bless others. To my regret, I've had to learn some of the truths the hard way.

Every dad wants a basketball hoop at the end of the driveway. It's a requirement of parental passage to prove you are committed to providing the best for your kids! I am no exception, so my son and I set out one Saturday to find the right kit. The next stop was the hardware store for a bag of cement. Thirty minutes later, I was pounding a posthole digger into the ground, and pouring wet cement around the apparatus that would soon stand proudly in its place: a gleaming monument to father-son togetherness.

But that's not exactly the way it turned out. As someone well said, "The road to hell is paved with good intentions." As laudable as my intentions may have been, I found it difficult to find the time to join Joe Jr. for after-school hoops.

To begin with, there was the lawn….

I have always been obsessed with having a well-trimmed, weedless, green-to-the-death kind of lawn. I am lost in a happy glow whenever I am cutting, trimming, fertilizing, and standing back to admire my artistry. (I know, I'm not well.) Given my need to manicure my lawn to the max, I invested my rare evenings at home in grass world, letting my son's frequent requests for games of one-on-one and H-O-R-S-E go mostly unheeded.

In addition to my landscape obsession, I was pastoring a church at that time. And that meant unscheduled crises and emergencies that soaked up what little discretionary time was left in my schedule. I'll never forget the day I was called to the hospital to sit with one of our families. Their son, about the age of my son, was hanging in the balance between life and death. We waited, prayed, and hoped for the best. But it was not to be. Their son died that afternoon.

As I was driving home from the hospital my values went through a wash of guilt. *What if it had been my boy? What if it had been Joe Jr.?* The pain that gripped my chest in that moment was so real I felt as if it could have been my Joe in that hospital. My Joe on the way to the funeral home.

As I turned down our street, my yard was the envy of the neighborhood. Deep emerald green. Its edges ruler straight. Its smooth expanse free of weeds. Like a golf course. Like a poster for a home and garden show. No one's lawn topped mine. Pulling into my driveway, the first thing I saw was the lonely basketball hoop, casting its long shadow across that picture-perfect grass.

And my heart sank like a stone.

Sitting in my car, staring at the quiet backboard and net, I suddenly hated my lawn. Every after-work hour spent on that pitiful square of turf had robbed me of valuable time I could have spent with my son. I was sick inside that I could have been so shallow to be distracted from what was truly important in life by grass. Grass that as soon as winter arrived would look as lame as the rest of the withered lawns on the street. How much better it would have been to pave it over with concrete and paint it green, rather than neglect never-to-be-redeemed time with my boy.

There was still some daylight left in that warm summer evening, so I rushed into the house and called to him. "Joe? You here? Want to play some one-on-one?" From his room, through the door, I heard the crushing words. "Sorry, Dad, I can't come now. I'm busy." (Thankfully, my son and I are now closer than ever. He and I not only play a lot of golf together, but he beats me unmercifully!)

But this may be a good time for me to throw out a question. *What are the lawns in your life?* Your hobby? Your career? Your easy evenings in the swivel chair? Your social life with that "in crowd"? Your dreams for all that is bigger and better, newer and faster?

I don't know what your lawns are. I just know that we all have them!

And who is it in your life whose needs have been eclipsed by the withering grass of life on your own terms? A friend in need? Your wife? Your husband? Your children? A neighbor in need? A colleague at work? A widow? An orphan?

In Peter's terms, it wasn't the lawn, it was fish.

He had traded his great potential to take the healing, rescuing, encouraging, and liberating gifts of grace to people in his world…for fish. Fish were a way to take care of himself, to meet his own needs. They were easier. More predictable. More what he liked to do. More what he thought was necessary!

But Jesus was not ready to let Peter go.

And He's not ready to let you go, either.

Jesus' first question to Peter has an interesting twist. "Simon, son of John, do you love Me more than these?" (John 21:15).

More than who? More than what? At first thought it would seem that Jesus was asking Peter if he loved Him more than Thomas or James or John did. But that is highly unlikely. Jesus had never been pleased by the competitiveness among His disciples—which one of them would be greatest in the kingdom, etc. At that weighty moment, it is doubtful He would want to launch another contest of comparison.

What, then, was Christ saying when He asked about loving Him more than these?

There was only one thing left on the beach.

The fish! One hundred fifty-three scaly, smelly fish!

Did Peter love fish—did he love his old life, his old ways, his old comforts—more than he loved His Lord?

I can't imagine Peter saying at this point, "Actually, Lord, I like You a lot but I really am into fish at this stage of my life!" Of course not. But I do wonder if that is what Jesus hears from our hearts as He challenges us about living out our love for Him into the lives of others.

Did you ever wonder why Jesus selected Peter out of all of them to interrogate in such a penetrating way? Didn't the others count? Didn't Jesus care if they loved Him? Of course He cared. But Peter had been the instigator. It was his idea to set aside the enterprise of the kingdom for nets and bobbers. But as they all sat there on the beach, finishing up their fish sandwiches, totally absorbed in the conversation between Peter and their Lord, you can bet they got the point. It's like spanking your oldest child; the younger ones shape up without a word. Peter was pivotal.

What I find fascinating and particularly helpful is the context into which these questions are spoken. In the story, Jesus challenges Peter's "bail-out" attitude on three fronts. Each one is intended to transition Peter from fishing to the enterprise of people. These three dynamics create steps for us as well. Steps back to a love for Jesus that touches His heart and blesses those who cross the path of our existence.

1. EMBRACE THE CALL AGAIN.

Peter and the rest of his crew had fished all night and caught nothing. (I can hardly resist noting that when we launch out in life on our own terms, it inevitably amounts to a disappointing catch!) I wonder if, as dawn broke across the still sea and mist rolled off the hills, those discouraged disciples flashed back to other scenes so fresh in their minds. On those very hills surrounding the lake, Jesus had healed the sick, fed the five thousand, and taught with spellbinding authority. The memories of days gone by must have weighed heavy on their hearts.

But over on the shore, a moving figure caught their eye. A man. Another fisherman, perhaps? A lonely beachcomber, taking a morning walk? They had no idea that it was their resurrected Lord.

The stranger on the shore shouted to them over the water. What was he saying? Ah yes, the typical "Any luck?" sort of question. Perhaps slightly irritated at the query (and embarrassed to admit that they'd had no luck at all), they shouted back a simple "No!"

The stranger then suggested they throw the net on the other side of the boat, and…you know the rest of the story. In a moment of brilliance, John said to Peter, "It's the Lord!"

At that point the text says that Peter put on his robe and jumped overboard (again), sloshing through the shallows to meet Jesus on the shore.

Why was it Peter who went overboard? Why the rush to Jesus while the others rowed the boat ashore, dragging the nets overflowing with flopping fish?

Because the Man on shore had just repeated a signature

miracle with haunting significance for Peter. How could he forget that day when three years earlier, the Teacher stepped into his boat and asked him to row out a little way from shore while He taught the crowds? When the teaching was over, the Rabbi asked him how fishing had been. Peter admitted that business was not too good. They had "fished all night and caught nothing." In response, Jesus said, "Put out into the deep water and let down your nets for a catch" (Luke 5:4). Luke goes on to tell us that…

> When they had done this, they enclosed a great quantity of fish; and their nets began to break; so they signaled to their partners in the other boat for them to come and help them. And they came and filled both of the boats, so that they began to sink. (vv. 6–7)

Stunned and afraid, Peter fell on his face in the bottom of the boat at Jesus' feet, pleading, "Depart from me, for I am a sinful man, O Lord!" (v. 8). It was then that he heard those words that would define his calling—and the rest of his life: "Do not fear, from now on you will be catching men" (v. 10).

And now, in the very moment of Peter's backward slide into his pre-calling life, Jesus showed up on the beach with the identical miracle. Struck by the memory of his life-changing encounter with Christ three years earlier, Peter hurried back to Jesus to rekindle the call afresh.

Can you remember when you first came to Jesus, and felt the healing, cleansing touch of His liberating grace? When you told Him you would follow Him and embrace His cause and live to serve His mission? It might be good to ask yourself, what has changed? Has Jesus changed? Is His mission of no present value? Have the needs of people around your life changed?

Or have *you* changed?

What would it take for you in this moment to bow your head and embrace the call as though it were as new today? Jesus will meet you, right here in the pages of this book. If you let Him, He will rekindle a love for Him in your inner being that is so deep and true you will gladly join Him once more in the business He takes more seriously than anything else: rescuing, redeeming, and nurturing people.

Step one in answer to Jesus' final question is to *embrace the call again!*

2. BRING YOUR FAILURES TO HIM.

In a real sense, Peter was not the same man who had first encountered the power and authority of Christ in his fishing boat five feet from shore. Since that time, he had failed repeatedly. And just days before the climactic encounter on the beach, he had done the very thing he had sworn he would never do. Would rather die than do.

He had betrayed His Lord, denying Him in the face of ridiculing enemies. How astounding that Jesus would even want to show up and still be interested in Peter's love and partnership! But there He was. Standing on the shore. Waiting. Wanting Peter back.

In the Bible, even the smallest details can be significant. Such is the case with the notation in John 21:9 that Jesus had built a charcoal fire on the beach. It seems strange that John would have included such an insignificant detail. Why not just say that Jesus had built a fire? Who cares what fueled it?

Peter would have cared. For very good reason.

The word *charcoal* is used only twice in all the New Testament. One instance is here, along the shore of the Sea of Tiberias. And the only other instance (do you remember?) was in Caiaphas's courtyard…at the fire where Peter warmed himself as he disavowed any relationship to his suffering Friend.

Charcoal… Aromas have a way of bringing back memories, don't they? Burning leaves in the fall recall dozens of childhood memories for me. The smell of fresh cut grass reminds me of golf. Catching a whiff of your mother's favorite perfume as someone walks by triggers all kinds of thoughts about home and growing up.

I can't help but think that the pungent smell of that charcoal fire flooded Peter's heart with thoughts about his recent failure. By any other reasonable standard, that act of cowardice should have disqualified him for any future association with Christ or His people.

That's what you would think.

But that's not what Jesus thought.

In the eyes of Christ, Peter's collapse did not disqualify him from being forgiven and useable again for kingdom service. I can't help but believe that Jesus not only needed Peter to get back on calling, but that He missed His impulsive friend, and took the initiative to welcome him back. Even in the face of miserable failure.

Jesus knows. He knows your failures, your disabling weaknesses, your secret idolatries. He is fully aware of how you have blown it with people in the past. Nothing, not one detail, escapes His notice. Even so, He wants to cleanse and use you. He longs for your love again. Come just as you are and let Him lead you in the paths of righteousness. Come and go with Him to the needs and nurture of people.

After all, if He wasn't interested in failures He would have no followers.

The words of a hymn I grew up singing form a fitting prayer: *"Stoop to my weakness, mighty as Thou art, and help me love You as I ought to love!"*

Step two in answer to His final question is to *bring your failures to Him.* Regardless of who you are or where you have been, Jesus wants you back to the enterprise of the kingdom, cleansed and ready to make a difference in peoples' lives!

3. TRUST HIM TO PROVIDE.

There is one very tender, mostly overlooked detail in this story about the reunion on the beach.

In fact, it is a miracle.

We have already noted that one of the reasons Peter and the small band of other disciples went back into business for themselves was to provide for their own needs and desires. And that makes this often unnoticed miracle in our story very instructive.

When they landed on the beach, Jesus had already laid a charcoal fire and was grilling fish on it. *Where did those fish come from?* The Jesus who had no boat and no net had made a miraculous catch of His own.

Why?

Because Jesus wanted to make a very strategic point—to them, and to all of us who find ourselves distracted from mission by our own needs and wants.

Jesus is the provider! As we serve Him, He will provide

for us spiritually, physically, materially, and in every way. And He will do so *generously*. It's obvious that John, who is telling us this story, is a fisherman. He tells us how many fish there are in their nets. One hundred fifty-three of them. And note that he also adds they are "large" fish. Far from being a net full of mere "keepers," these were trophies! Our Lord's grace is not only sufficient, He is able to provide exceedingly abundantly above all that we ask or think. And as He had already told His disciples, if they would seek the kingdom, all their needs would be cared for. As He said, "Your Father knows you have need of these things."

You may go off mission for personal gain or to meet your own needs, but it is never a reason. Only an excuse.

Jesus provides!

He provides the grace that will sustain and revitalize you. When you don't know what to do next, He provides wisdom. When you have given yourself away to others, He will care for you with special fellowship with Him or through the love and care of another that He sends your way. When you are out of cash, He will supply the very resources you need. When you are pressed for time because you've given up several hours to help someone, He will make it up to you. It is our calling to serve. It is His joy to supply!

Step three toward an others-oriented life is to *get busy in the lives of men and women and trust God to provide and protect.*

Reclaim your calling as a follower! Come for cleansing and restoration from your past failures! Trust Him to supply for your needs as you give to the needs of others! And get busy. He will experience your love as you reach out to love others.

Chapter Fourteen

Caring About What He Cares About

...And seeing people in a whole new light.

Waves lapped the shoreline, the charcoal glowed on the sand, and the rising sun melted away the night shadows.

A peaceful, tranquil setting, perhaps, but something extremely significant would happen on that lonely Galilee beach over two thousand years ago. Jesus was about to teach Peter an unforgettable lesson. And it was this: When you turn your back on people, you in essence have turned your back on Jesus.

This is a landmark point for those of us who are still saying, "Give me one really good reason to inconvenience my life by reaching out to people!" The really good reason is that you intervene in people's lives not for their sake—or even yours—but to demonstrate the depth and quality of your love for Jesus.

Let's unwrap Jesus' conversation with Peter. Perhaps we can pick up a clue or two to help us engage with fresh enthusiasm the wild, wonderful, sometimes bewildering world of people.

Let's go back to John 21, and the drama that unfolded after that early morning fish fry on the beach. At the end of Christ's ministry on earth, He showed up one more time to intercept the disoriented lives of His disciples. His purpose was to direct them back on track for His intended purpose for their lives. His target on this occasion was Peter…but it might as well have been you or me.

> So when they had finished breakfast, Jesus said to Simon Peter, "Simon, son of John, do you love Me more than these?" He said to Him, "Yes, Lord; You know that I love You." He said to him, "Tend My lambs."
>
> He said to him again a second time, "Simon, son of John, do you love Me?" He said to Him, "Yes, Lord; You know that I love You." He said to him, "Shepherd My sheep."

He said to him the third time, "Simon, son of John, do you love Me?" Peter was grieved because He said to him the third time, "Do you love Me?" And he said to Him, "Lord, You know all things; You know that I love You." Jesus said to him, "Tend My sheep." (John 21:15–17)

What was Jesus getting at here? Was He questioning the depth of Peter's love? That's what I'd been taught for years. In fact, I've probably preached sermons from that perspective. A little secret locked in the Greek text is that Peter and Jesus used two different words for love in that exchange. Jesus asked Peter if he *agaped* Him. And Peter answered, "Yes, Lord, I *phileo* You!"

Agape love is the highest kind of love, used most often to describe God's love for us. It is a love that transcends feelings, environment, personal interests, and worthiness to receive it. *Agape* loves willingly—regardless. It is unconditional and absolutely reliable.

Phileo love, on the other hand, is a kind of family love—a brotherly love. It's how you feel about your brother or sister (after you are twenty-five!).

Since Jesus repeats the question, it is easy to assume He is trying to ratchet up Peter's love from the *phileo* level to the higher level of *agape*. Hence, He asks the question a second time. As though Jesus was saying, "Now Peter, listen carefully to what I'm saying...do you *agape* Me?" The problem with this approach is that in the third round of questioning Jesus uses the *phileo* word. Is Jesus then saying, "Well, all right, I'll settle for *phileo* love if that's all you can give Me"? It's just like Jesus to lower the bar of commitment, right? Of course not! I've never known Him to do that.

In fact, the words *agape* and *phileo* are on rare occasion used interchangeably. To Peter's credit, perhaps, he was saying that his love was something more than a love of determined choice. After three intensive years of deep bonding, he truly loved Jesus as a brother. In that culture, the bond of love between siblings was even more important than love for parents.

If the meaning is not in the words, then what's going on here? Why the extended interrogation? Some have speculated that since Peter denied Jesus three times just days earlier, Jesus is reminding Peter of that failure of love and loyalty.

Well, maybe. But in reality the text doesn't tell us why Jesus asked the question three times. What we are sure about, however, is that Jesus didn't accept the mere verbal affirmation of Peter's love. In each case, Jesus drove Peter right past his words *"I love you."* It would be the actions of Peter's life that would prove his love for Christ. And so it is for you and me.

Loving Jesus would mean *caring about what Jesus cared about*. And as we know, He cares first and foremost about people! Their needs and nurture. The welfare of their lives and their eternal destinies.

This may come as a disappointment to some of you, but I lived most of my early years in a non-pet family. The few pet memories that I retain are not all that compelling. I recall begging my parents for a puppy at Christmas, which we then gave away six weeks later because I'd neglected him. Then there was the Easter when someone in my dad's church gave us a bunch of baby chicks. My most vivid memory of that episode was watching my sister accidentally step on one. (I'll spare you the details.)

Come to think of it, my mother did keep a canary for years, but do you know how hard it is to bond with a bird?

So I grew up thinking pets were unnecessary and irrelevant. It was obvious, wasn't it? People who lacked human affection and couldn't make it through life on their own needed to be propped up by a pet. But for the rest of us well-balanced, self-sufficient individuals, pets were not a requirement.

Soon after we got married, however, Martie suggested that we get a dog. Clueless, I let fly with this "only people who can't make it with human relationships need the crutch of a pet" kind of talk. I'm afraid it wasn't my best moment. Nor did it move us to new heights in our fledgling relationship.

I had forgotten that Martie had grown up in a pet family. Her lifelong love was Trudy, a black retriever. Trudy was always there for her. If all her friends had rejected her at school, Trudy was there to welcome her home with tail-wagging affection. When Martie would close her bedroom door and have a good cry, Trudy would be there to lick the tears from her cheeks.

At that uncomfortable moment in our relationship, I had to come to grips with a very important principle: *You express your love to someone by caring about what they care about.*

So…we bought a dog. An Old English sheepdog that we named Paddington.

As it turned out, it wasn't the initial investment but the upkeep that would prove the depth of my love. Like it or not, this non-dog person would have to love the dog to communicate love for Martie.

So I fed her. Walked her late at night. Cleaned up after her. And wouldn't you know it? She began to steal a piece of my heart.

Paddington's arrival, however, and my subsequent com-

mitment to help Martie maintain and care for her had little
to do with the dog.

To me, it was all about Martie.

It was my love for her that engaged me in Dog World.
And to this day—though Paddington has gone on to the Big
Bone in the Sky—I have never regretted it.

In fact, as a result of learning that my love is proven by
"caring about what she cares about"—my life has been plunged
into any number of activities that quite frankly haven't been all
that much fun. I've hung miles of wallpaper, painted countless
rooms, changed diapers, dusted, and vacuumed. Loving
Martie means what it means in any other love relationship—
climbing into her world and caring about what she cares about.

That's exactly the point that Jesus is driving home in this
text. *If you love Me, you will care about what I care about.*

It can't be overlooked in our text that Jesus uses "sheep"
as a word picture for people.

If you know much about sheep at all, the imagery is highly
instructive. And not particularly flattering. Sheep are neither
strong, fast, or mentally swift. They are extremely vulnerable to
predators. They are wanderers and easily lose their way. In fact,
they can't even find their way home to the barn on their own
without a shepherd to guide them. (Which makes the advice
that someone gave to Little Bo Peep really lame! You know...

"Leave them alone, and they will come home, wagging their tails behind them." In her dreams, maybe!) Sheep tend to over-drink in fast moving waters, and since their nostrils and mouth are so close, can actually drown themselves in satisfying their thirst.

Quite simply, these are among the more mentally and directionally challenged members of the animal kingdom. They really need help.

Just like people.

People are vulnerable. And headstrong. And foolish. And weak. Apart from the protection of Christ, we are all easy marks for the defeating and debilitating attacks of the spiritual underworld. No matter how well educated, wealthy, or crafty one might be, even the best of us are out of our league when it comes to the forces of the evil one. We are like sheep in need of shepherding!

The point that Jesus was making is that people need help.

And that is what shepherds do.

They help.

They protect, sustain, and rescue sheep who have blundered into thorny thickets while nosing after greener grass.

They pursue little lambs (and old ewes and rams who ought to know better) who have been caught in the pits and snares of life.

Do I hear you thinking that this would be a really good thing for your *pastor* to read? After all, aren't they the shepherds of God's flock?

Well, yes. But it is not only them. Jesus calls all of His followers to shepherd and tend others. And if you think there may not be much glamour to it, you are exactly right. Shepherds of Jesus' day were at the low end of the social stratum. It was often a lonely, unheralded task. But sheep were the source of wealth. As weak and witless as they may have been, they were the backbone of their owner's financial portfolio. In that day, you measured your success and fortune by how many sheep you had, and what condition they were in. Seen from that perspective, shepherds were the stewards of the most valuable commodity in the land.

Get the point?

God's earthside wealth is measured in the valuable commodity of people. They are the only part of His creation that He created in His image. Why? So that He could be glorified through them and find fellowship and satisfaction in them. He has no more important possession. But His treasure is at risk, and we are the shepherds who care for His portfolio. When we do it well, He feels our love.

So here is the liberating truth: Getting involved with people in constructive ways isn't about them at all. It doesn't make any difference if you like them or not; if they deserve your attention or not; if your attention to them is rewarded or not; or even if they misunderstand and respond to your care in negative ways. It isn't really an issue if your wife rides in through the window on a broom, or if your husband's limp body is a fixture on the sofa with a remote surgically embedded in his hand. All of that is totally irrelevant, and can no longer count as a legitimate excuse for checking out of the people business.

You aren't doing it for *them*. You are doing it for Jesus, who *does* deserve all the love you can muster.

Now, I wouldn't recommend you tell people that your efforts to bless and benefit their lives has nothing to do with them. But that's the truth. In the end, it is Jesus and your heart's desire to please and honor Him that drives you into the arena with people. All kinds of people!

In my years of serving Christ at the Moody Bible Institute and as a pastor, I've had many different kinds of people cross my path. There wasn't one who didn't have some measure of need. In fact, it was quite evident that some were more needy than others. As a friend of mine is fond of saying, "The light always attracts a few bugs!" And quite frankly (if I might admit it to you as a kind of private confession), some of them caused great frustration—and often preoccupied my heart and mind with their criticisms and demands.

I'll never forget the new enthusiasm that lifted my spirits the day I realized that all of these people around my life—both the rewarding ones and the unrewarding—were precious to Jesus! And, *if they are precious to Jesus then they must be precious to me!* They are in fact His prized possessions. He died for each of them. He loves them and desires to lead them to the best...warts and all. And He is looking to me to love Him enough to help get the job done.

How nice it would be if you could "just love Jesus" without the messy, frustrating people-component. I've often thought my Christianity would be a cakewalk if it weren't for people!

Chapter Fifteen

The Priority of People

...No one said it would be easy.

Clutching his ever present blanket, and with unusual determination in his voice, Linus announced to Lucy he had finally discovered his calling in life. He was going to be a doctor.

Lucy, ever the intimidating big sister, countered that there was no way he could be a doctor because, as she said, he hated mankind.

Stung by that objection, Linus shot back that she really didn't understand. He *loved* mankind. It was people he couldn't stand.

All of us can identify with Linus's dubious distinction. Humankind is a wondrous thing. It's those pesky people who spoil the broth. While often the source of our greatest joys, people are just as likely to use us, frustrate us, cheat us, intimidate us, misunderstand us, criticize us, manipulate us, abuse us, talk behind our backs, ignore us, and inevitably disappoint us.

Most of us have come to realize that people are complex and unpredictable—especially if they're "not like us." Differences in gender, color, culture, and class complicate our desire to find pleasure in relationships. We find ourselves confused and overly cautious when the person who brings us delight in one moment disappoints us the next!

The only way to survive in this people-dangerous world (so we are told) is to take matters into our own hands and make sure that life is all about us—our own dreams, goals, and desires. And when people threaten the trajectory of those dreams, we should jettison them. As quickly as possible. Use those who can help you and eliminate everyone else seems to be the name of the game.

As Paul Simon used to sing, "Just slip out the back, Jack, and set yourself free."

In short, with the exception of several periodic casual and comfortable encounters, living for others—for their needs and nurture—seems far too hazardous. Some of us have learned the hard way that getting involved with people leaves us vulnerable and at risk. Outside of a few close friends who make us feel good about ourselves, and subordinates at work who do what we tell them to and treat us well (to our face), the world of people is often too spooky for us to wade in much further than the shallow end.

Masking our resistance to closer relationships, we salve our neglect by "focusing on Jesus." Sounds good, doesn't it? After all, He's the one we can trust. In relationship with Him (who needs people?), we feel safe, secure, and satisfied.

But we are also way off the mark. And the Lord of our lives is not pleased. Patiently, firmly, repeatedly, He keeps reminding us that our relationship with Him is going nowhere unless it is lived out in a bold, constructive involvement in the lives of others. When Peter affirmed his love for Jesus verbally, Jesus said in essence that He would know that Peter was serious about loving Him when Peter got busy with people. Or, as Jesus actually said it, "Feed My sheep." He measures His worth in our lives not by what we say, not by what we sing in heartfelt worship, not by how many rules we keep, but rather by how we treat people and respond to their needs.

One of the Sadducees' lawyers once sought to trap Jesus with a leading question. "Teacher," he asked, "which is the greatest commandment in the law?"

For His answer, Jesus reached all the way back to the first of the Ten Commandments: That we love the Lord our God with our heart, soul, and mind.

We all like that command. It has a nice ring to it. But then He upped the ante.

The second, He said, was like the first: You should love your neighbor as you love yourself. In other words, *If you say you love God, then the proof of that love rises and falls on what you do with and for your neighbor.*

You're probably saying, "Right, but obviously Jesus doesn't know my neighbor!"

Instead of assuming that the omniscience of Jesus stops at your property line, it would be better if you asked, "Who is my neighbor?"

Brace yourself.

The biblical definition of neighbor, as Jesus uses it in this text, is *anyone who crosses the path of your life*—not just the guy or gal who occupies the space next door. It's that rude person in the "12 Items or Less" line at the grocery store, who makes you late because he has just placed 17 items on the belt. (And you know there are 17 items because you counted them one by one!)

It's your wife. Your husband. Your roommate. Your coworker. It's anyone who comes close enough to be loved and helped.

In His last teaching session with His disciples, Jesus raised the bar even higher with a new command: that they love one another. Surely at a bare minimum, that means we need to get positively involved in the lives of fellow followers. And let's face it, this may be the toughest test yet. Do you ever feel that many people you know who are outside the faith are nicer and easier to love than some of the Christians you know? I'm reminded of the ditty that goes, "To live above with saints we love, oh that will be glory. To live below with saints we know...well, that's a different story!"

But the real issue comes to the surface when Jesus adds this reminder: Others outside of the family will only recognize our link to Him if we live to love each other. That's a good reminder for those of us who for too long have thought that outsiders will know we are Christians because "we don't drink, dance, smoke, chew, or go with girls who do."

After teaching some of these concepts in this book a few months ago, I was approached by a lady after the session. She told me that she and her husband had recently begun attending a small church. Their new fellowship, she noted, put a heavy emphasis on conformity to a list of "lifestyle" rules as long as your arm. Yet at the same time, she added, she had never been in a church where there was more gossip and backstabbing going on.

You can take it to the bank that Jesus is not loved in that place—regardless of what they say or sing, regardless of what

Bible translation they preach from the pulpit, regardless of whether their list of rules reaches around the block and back.

Ask yourself this simple question: "What is the primary concern of my life?" For some, the honest answer is personal survival. For others, answers like saving for retirement, making more money, getting ahead at work, snagging that "ideal" date, spending a quiet evening by the fire with a good book, or improving a golf handicap may head the list. The reality is that unconditionally intervening in others' lives to help and heal probably doesn't rank near the top of most of our lists.

And, I would like to add, there is probably nothing wrong with the things on your list. I really do hope to improve my golf handicap! It's just that there is something wrong with any list that does not feature the priority of people at the top.

If you are still wondering if this is really all that important, think of what James says. *The Message* paraphrase puts it like this: "Anyone who sets himself up as 'religious' by talking a good game is self-deceived. This kind of religion is hot air and only hot air. Real religion, the kind that passes muster before God the Father, is this: Reach out to the homeless and loveless in their plight, and guard against corruption from the godless world" (James 1:26–27).

We need to get a grip on the reality that following Jesus

is not always just about "us and Him"; nor is it always a safe and comfortable thing. Yes, it is always a good and ultimately rewarding endeavor to follow Him. But be ready: That path will always lead directly into the lives of others.

At this point I am sure that a lot of objections are surfacing in your heart. Don't be surprised. The adversary wants people for his own destructive purposes without your getting in the way. I know the excuses, because at one time or another, I've been tempted to use them all myself. *He doesn't deserve my care and attention.... Anyway, if I'm nice to her, she'll take advantage of me.... My acts of help will most likely be misunderstood, rejected, criticized, ignored, or unsuccessful.... Besides, what about ME? Who will care for and love me if I start to prioritize the needs of others in my life?... Besides, honestly, I'm usually too tired after I've given it all at the office to do much else besides channel surf in my easy chair.*

No one said it would be easy. In fact, Jesus got involved in the needs of your life and mine all the way to the cross. Which reminds me that when He calls us to follow Him, He also says that we are to take up our cross as well.

Remember! We are not home yet. We are at war, and running rescue operations into the world of people is going to take grit. But as Hebrews tells us, Jesus persevered in the ordeal to rescue our perishing souls for the joy that was set before Him. Think of a brother won, a sister rescued from a fall, the smile on an orphan's face, a friend encouraged, and your six-year-old son hugging your neck and saying, "Dad, I love it when you play ball with me!" The struggle may be periodically challenging, but the rewards are out of this world!

One of my fondest memories as a boy took place late at night after my dad had prayed with me and turned out the lights. I had rescued a discarded old radio and placed it on the nightstand by my bed. After waiting for my dad to get down the hall, I'd turn it on with the volume way down low. By sliding my pillow over to the edge of the bed, I was able to listen with no one else knowing. Into the darkness, a calm and soothing voice would begin his program by singing these words…

Somebody cares about you,
And worries till the day comes shining through!
Somebody cares if you sleep well at night,
If your day goes all wrong,
Or if your day goes all right!
Somebody cares about you,
And worries till the sun comes shining through.
Please believe me, it's so, But in case you didn't
   know it,
Somebody cares!

Then he would always say, *"Have no fear, Big Joe is here!"* During the rest of the program, Big Joe took calls from people in need, and arranged ways for their needs to be met.

To my little uncomplicated life, there was a soothing and nourishing feeling in my spirit when I heard Big Joe sing and talk. To me, he seemed like a huge, oversized, soft marshmallow that all the world could fall into and be happy.

Since I grew up just outside of New York City, it strikes me now, as an adult, that in such a large and impersonal city many were lost and alone, overwhelmed by needs in their lives. How healing it must have been to them to hear that somebody cared!

There may even be someone reading this book right now who is holding back the tears, wishing that someone would read these pages and intervene in their lives in a caring way.

Could it be you that they are waiting for?

Chapter Sixteen

So Many People, So Little Time

Committing intentional acts of love

Here is what we have learned. From Jesus' point of view, only one thing really counts in this world.

People.

God's Son is passionate about rescuing men and women, boys and girls, from the evil designs of the destroyer. He cares about their daily lives and their struggles. He cares about their eternal destiny.

He wept over Jerusalem because He would have gathered them as vulnerable chicks under His wings. He was moved with compassion because, as He saw it, people were distressed and dismayed…like sheep without a shepherd. With His own lips He declared His reason for visiting our broken planet: "For the Son of Man has come to seek and to save that which was lost" (Luke 19:10). Life was never about Him. He didn't have long here, and rescue was always on His mind. If you doubt it, just follow Him.

All the way to the cross.

Outside of stepping aside periodically to rest and pray to re-tank His strength for another run at people, His life was never absorbed with His own interests or making a mark for Himself. In His own words, "The Son of Man did not come to be served, but to serve, and to give His life a ransom for many" (Matthew 20:28).

I don't ever recall Him saying to Judas, His CFO, "Do we have enough money to buy that hill over there? It would make a great place for a Messianic Library after I die, so that people will remember Me and the contribution I have made."

His life was singularly focused on people. He knew better than anyone else that the only commodity at risk in the unseen warfare—and the only entity going all the way into eternity—is people. He was well aware that everything else gets checked at the border.

He lived to prove one profound point: *Only people count.* And He wants His followers to share His passion and to partner in His mission. When we do, He knows how much we love Him!

So let's connect the dots. First of all let's remind ourselves that we're certainly not lacking in prospects! People are everywhere. The bumper sticker motto of every follower of Jesus ought to be, "So many people, so little time!"

But beware of being too narrow in the target zone of your efforts. Always keep in mind that God's Son reached out to those who were despised, condemned, and hated by seemingly everyone else. He stood beside the woman caught in adultery, as one by one her accusers melted away. He attended parties with hated tax collectors, heavy imbibers, and known prostitutes. He opened His heart and the very doors of heaven to the convicted felon dying on the cross next to His. And not so very long later, He sought out, received, and commissioned Saul of Tarsus, a committed enemy and persecutor of the church.

Jesus took hit after hit for caring about the needs and welfare of those who were considered nonpersons or worse to the religious elite. He didn't write anyone off—unless it was those haughty religious leaders who stubbornly clung to their proud and hypocritical righteousness. Jesus continually stunned His friends and foes alike by the company He kept. When He saw the slightest spark, the slightest inclination toward God-hunger in an individual's soul, nothing else mattered. Not race. Not gender. Not status. Not track record. Not public opinion. Not multiplied failures.

In many respects, caring about people is a calling without boundaries. And the issue is not that you go out of your way and dismantle your priorities to find some rejected soul. It simply means that your heart remains open to whomever it is that God leads across your path. And if that man or woman happens to walk outside the normal standards of decency and propriety, you refuse to back away. Instead, you let the love of Jesus flow through your life with intention and resolve.

Are you ready now to engage your world for Jesus? Great. But hold up just for a moment. There are a few simple rules of engagement that you need to keep in mind.

1. YOU CAN'T HELP EVERYONE ALL THE TIME!

It's important to know yourself and to know your limits. Even Jesus left some unhealed and unhelped.

2. ESTABLISH YOUR PRIORITIES.

For what people are you directly responsible? You can't neglect them for the needs of others. There are concentric circles of care. At the center is your spouse (or, if you are single, it may be a close friend). The next circle represents your children, then your extended family, then your brothers and sisters in Christ, then others who cross your path at work or in the normal course of your daily routine.

3. STEP AWAY WHEN YOU ARE DRAINED.

You can't minister from an empty tank. Even Jesus went apart to rest awhile. When your tank registers on "Weary," find a way to refresh yourself. And then step back into the people business with new resolve.

4. BE AWARE OF YOUR CAPACITY TO HELP.

Know yourself! Some of us are not equipped to help with in-depth counseling, mental or emotional illness, financial advice, or serious health concerns. There are "holders," "helpers," and "healers" in the body of Christ. Sometimes we can just hold on to people until we can find someone to help them. At others times we can offer limited help until we can get them to someone who can heal them. And sometimes we get the opportunity to do all three.

5. KNOW THAT THERE ARE SOME PEOPLE WHO WILL NEVER BE HELPED.

Unfortunately, there are a few people who have learned that the only way to get attention and to feel loved is to have a problem. If that is the case, you can never help them, because their problem is their treasure. If you have spent a lot of time and there are seemingly no improvements or any response to healthy counsel, then you need to graciously bow out and invest your time and talents elsewhere.

In the context of these boundaries, what do you have in your hand? What resources do you bring with which to engage people at their point of need? If you are saying, "Not much," then let me remind you of the boy who brown-bagged it to a revival service. All he had was a little lunch with two fish and five loaves. And, by the way, these were most likely small biscuits of barley and salted dried fish the size of sardines. It wasn't much. But as the old saying goes, "Little is much when God is in it!" Put whatever resource you possess in His hands, and watch it multiply.

Let me suggest some of the resources that every one of us has in our personal bag of need-meeting power.

1. PRAYER

I put this first because I'm guessing it might be at the *bottom* of your list—if it made it at all. Periodically someone will ask me, "What can I do to help?" And when I can't come up with anything off the top of my head, they will often say, "Well, I'll just pray." *Just* pray? You must be kidding. Prayer is the power that moves God's heart.

Each summer over three thousand Christians descend on a rather sleepy town in the Lake District of the UK known as Keswick, actually doubling the size of the town. They come for three weeks of worship and study of the Word at Britain's most historic conference grounds.

Last summer I was asked to participate in the teaching sessions of the first week of the Keswick conference. I started the assignment on Sunday morning by preaching in one of the churches at the outskirts of town. The pastor had asked one of the ladies in the church to come and lead in prayer, and then give her testimony. It all seemed normal enough...until she began to share how she came to know Christ as her Savior.

She told the congregation that she worked in a deli/gift shop in Keswick. Several years previous, during one of the Keswick weeks, a lady attending the conference came into the shop every morning for coffee, and struck up a friendship with her. She admitted that there was something different about this woman, and that at the end of the week she felt sorry that her new friend, Winnie, was leaving to go back to her home. Every year she waited to see Winnie again during the conference weeks, but as the years passed she never came back.

Several years after she had met Winnie, however, she began to have a drawing in her spirit to Jesus that was so strong—so irresistible—that it was almost physical in its power. After trying to dismiss it, she found that it persisted in increasing strength, until one day she wandered into a church. After meeting with the pastor, she accepted the Lord Jesus as her Savior.

A couple of years later, a lady walked into the shop during the conference weeks and asked her if she remembered Winnie from many years before. She lit up at the thought of her long-absent friend, and said that she certainly did remember. She added that long after she had met Winnie, she had come to know Christ as her Lord and Savior! The lady on the other side of the counter gasped in joy, and said she couldn't wait to tell Winnie, *since Winnie had prayed for her salvation every day without fail since she left Keswick years before.*

I could hardly hold back the tears as I listened to this testimony. Every day! Praying and praying for someone you had met years before, until the enemy finally said, "I give up, I can't hold on to her against the power of these persistent prayers." And the way was cleared for Jesus to energize her heart to come to Him.

Then to cap it all off she said, "And I am so glad that Winnie is here this morning," at which point warrior-hero

Winnie stood up to the enthusiastic applause of that typically staid English congregation.

As we walked out, I saw her with Winnie walking down the lane and hurried to catch up. Telling them what an encouragement her testimony had been to me, I added that since it took so many years for Winnie's prayer to be answered, Satan must have had a tight grip on this shopkeeper's life. She looked at me with a serious and telling look and said, "I cannot tell you how strong his grip was on my life!"

Winnie is a model of what it means to be undauntedly faithful to the call of rescuing men and women. She persevered in long-distance prayer without a clue of what was going on in the spiritual underworld. The Spirit energized her undaunted commitment to the welfare of others and the battle was won.

Can you in this quiet moment think of a person who rises as a candidate for your first redemptive move?

2. YOUR SPIRITUAL GIFT

All who have come to Jesus as Savior have been endowed with a special gift to empower and enable you for service. This gift is to be used to bless and help others. There are gifts of *serving, hospitality, mercy, giving, administration, teaching, exhortation, prophecy, etc.* Your gift is your ability to play a constructive role for Christ's sake in the lives of others. But finding and knowing that gift is often a challenge. Someone wisely counseled me years ago that you can know what your gift is by the kind of activity you are naturally drawn to, that you have energy for, that you see fruitfulness in, and that others affirm you in when you exercise it. The way to discover your spiritual gift is to get busy in the people business until you can sense where you are most effective. Don't try to serve apart from your lead gift. It is defeating to try to do things that you are not built to do.

3. TIME AND ATTENTION

We all have the capacity to give both of these commodities away on a regular basis. The most flattering service that a husband and father can give to his wife and kids is his time and attention.

Give a day a month to some enterprise that is effectively helping and reaching people. Ladle soup at the mission. Paint a widow's living room. Change the storm windows for a disabled person. There are lots of opportunities in this category.

4. MONEY

Most of us do not have the giftedness, calling, or capacity to minister to the homeless, AIDS victims, the disabled, and the orphaned. But that does not mean that we cannot have a part in their need. Pick a ministry that targets and effectively serves and blesses these categories of people. Partner with them in prayer and regular financial support. For years Martie and I have split our giving into two categories. We give our tithe to our local church and then have what we call our "Special Giving" fund. This extra fund gives us the freedom to save a significant amount of resources to bless and help as needs arise. Try it. It brings us a lot of joy.

5. GRACE

Grace is the action of abundant kindness, even to the most undeserving of offenders. Grace forgives, gives space, and doesn't keep score. How is it that we who have been so greatly graced by God are so unwilling to give His grace to others? The most helpful thing you might do today is give someone the love they don't deserve.

6. ENCOURAGEMENT

Sometimes it's real simple and not very demanding. A word of comfort and hope. A call. A card. A passage of Scripture. A hug with no words. A listening ear. An understanding heart.

Can you in the quiet moment think of a person who rises as a candidate for your first redemptive move? There are people all around our lives who need the Lord—and will only find Him through us. There are people who need to be for-given so that they can have a future, rather than remaining imprisoned to the past. There are people who need to be cared for, in Jesus' name, just as He cares for us. There are people who need to be taken by the hand and led from addictive paths of darkness to the freedom of walking in His light. There are people who need to be strengthened and encouraged. There are people who need to be protected, restored to family and friends, and made to feel whole and valued. Never doubt it: These kinds of people are all around our lives every day.

How close are they? As close as your best Christian friend. As close as your own spouse.

One of the most moving scenes for me in the last movie of the epic *Lord of the Rings* trilogy was when Frodo collapsed on the very slopes of Mount Doom. So near the end of a long, long journey, with their destination at last in view, the ring bearer could go no further. With victory so close at hand in a great battle of good against evil, the forces of evil were about to win. Frodo's faithful companion, Sam, pleaded with his friend to get up and keep going—to finish the task before it was too late. When his fellow hobbit wouldn't or couldn't stir, Sam, himself exhausted beyond words, said, "Mr. Frodo, I can't do it for you, but I can pick you up and take you there."

Struggling, Sam picked Frodo up and carried him to the heart of Mount Doom, where victory would finally be won.

At one time or another, each of us needs a Sam. We need someone to be there to rescue us at the brink of failure, to communicate confidence and worth in the face of impending defeat and discouragement.

When Martie and I saw *The Return of the King*, I was going through a particularly challenging time, and found myself often plagued with confusing, disheartening thoughts and feelings. Since people have this weird sense that people who do what I do don't wrestle with discouragement, I often feel deeply alone in times like these. When my heart is down, I feel that I have far more critics than champions, and I find my spirit longing for a champion to carry and wave my flag. (I know that Jesus is my champion, but there are times when you need Him to incarnate His love and care in the skin of a fellow believer.) Perhaps that's why I identified so quickly with Sam's loving willingness to carry the battle-weary Frodo.

I so desperately wanted and needed a Sam!

I had been sharing with Martie some of my internal struggle just the day before, and her input had been a great help. As we walked from the theater, I said, "I feel like I need a Sam."

She grabbed my arm and pulled me close. With delight in her eyes and voice, she said, "I'm your Sam!"

I will never forget the depth of meaning that her words and the love in her eyes had on my heart. The person who knew me and loved me more than anyone else had just pledged herself afresh to lift me up and strengthen me for the journey. Just knowing that was a wind of healing to my soul. I was not alone!

Think of what God said to Israel: "The LORD your God carried you, just as a man carries his son, in all the way which you have walked until you came to this place.... Even to your old age...I will carry you...and I will deliver you" (Deuteronomy 1:31; Isaiah 46:4).

Actually our calling to get involved in redemptive ways in people's lives is nothing more than the high privilege of being to others what God is to us—what He would be to them if He were here in physical presence.

As you read these words on this page, all kinds of people are fighting all kinds of battles with the enemy of their soul. And they are waiting for the supernatural rescue Jesus seeks to offer them through us.

Have you ever wondered why you got stuck with so many weird and troublesome people in and around your life? God may have placed you, as His frontline soldier, on a frontier where a breakthrough of divine love would make all the difference. As you allow Him to rescue and love and shepherd through you, you may find yourself participating in a most dramatic victory against the underworld. You get to be the warrior hero!

Don't flinch at that designation. There is a lot at stake here. And thankfully, you don't do it alone. *All you do is to remain faithful to the call to live for the care and rescue of people.* For His part, the Spirit of God will energize your obedience to victory! Welcome back to the world of people!

Jesus & You...
Going Somewhere

If you are anything like me, you've read a lot of books that you've never finished. So (unless you're the kind of person who reads the last chapter first), thanks for getting all the way through this one.

I've heard authors before talk about praying for their readers, and I've always taken it with a grain of salt. Was it just nice talk, a pleasant thing to say, or did the author actually mean it?

I really do.

I'm praying specifically and passionately that the contents of this book gets through to the deepest parts of your inner being and helps you to refocus on what really counts in life.

And what is that?

You know what I'll say already.

What really counts is Jesus and your love for Him translated into acts of loving kindness toward those who intersect your life.

Following Jesus takes us places we never thought we

would go and into the pleasure of experiencing Him in ways that fully and finally satisfy.

So once again, I'm praying—actually praying—for you, my reader. I'm asking God (and He knows who you are) that your time spent in the pages of this book will motivate you to exit the hall of mirrors—where life is all about you—and into the fresh air of a new season in your life.

While it's important to get up close and personal with Jesus, we need to remember that intimacy with Him is something more than sitting on the porch with Him as the sun sets and the cool evening breezes blow.

Jesus is going somewhere...and that somewhere is right into the lives of people. And He's counting on you to be His hands and His healing touch on their lives.

Usually loving Jesus is in the form of one person's need at a time. But don't just stand there...love this Jesus that you long to experience...by intentionally loving someone today.

Dr. Joseph M. Stowell serves as the president of Cornerstone University in Grand Rapids, Michigan. An internationally recognized conference speaker, Joe has also written numerous books.

His life is marked by a deep love for Jesus, which is reflected in his desire to value people regardless of gender, race, or class; to aid the poor and marginalized; to build a strong and vibrant community where the presence of Christ is evident; and to govern and lead in ways that engender mutual confidence and trust.

Joe also works with RBC Ministries in Grand Rapids, partnering in media productions. His web ministry, Strength for the Journey, features daily devotionals, weekly messages and commentary, downloadable Bible study curriculum, and an audio library of his most requested messages.

Joe serves on the board of the Billy Graham Evangelistic Association and has a distinguished career in higher education and church leadership. He served as the president of Moody Bible Institute, and as teaching pastor at the 10,000-member Harvest Bible Chapel in suburban Chicago prior to assuming the presidency at Cornerstone University.

He is a graduate of Cedarville University and Dallas Theological Seminary and was honored with a doctor of divinity degree from The Masters College. Joe and his wife, Martie, have three children and several grandchildren.

Printed in the United States
by Baker & Taylor Publisher Services